What Your Colleagues Are Saying . . .

"You feel exhausted hearing all the roles of a leader: aspirers of high expectations and great ambitions, builders of collectives of learners and professional development, social influencers among leaders and teachers, leaders of teaching and learning, those who apply principles of improvement, amplifiers of effective instruction, architects of productive and inviting climates, beacons of trust, supporters of clarity about purpose and instruction, chief engagement officers of teacher and student learners, evaluators of impact, accountability officers, leaders of improvement, implementation scientists, and great managers. The alternative is a school of independent contractors where great teaching and leadership are by chance. *How Leadership Works* makes a convincing case about how to bring all these roles to fruition and how to have time left over to enjoy the success of all in the school (as well as your own successes)."

—**John Hattie,** Author, University of Melbourne

"To enhance your skills as a teacher of teachers, *How Leadership Works: A Playbook for Instructional Leaders* invites you to be an engaged learner. If you are looking for a nightstand book to passively peruse before sleep, this is not the book for you. If you are ready to roll up your sleeves and invest in some serious reflection about your own leadership practices around a powerful set of ideas, then dig in! This book is organized around a set of modules that include learning intentions and success criteria, vignettes, research-based practices, and space for reflection on what you will *keep, stop,* or *start* doing with what you have learned. It includes a variety of learning tools that will not only support you in your learning but will become a valuable set of tools for you to use as you support the thinking and learning of the teachers you lead. In the end, the thinking and learning of your students will blossom and grow."

—**Megan Tschannen-Moran,** Professor of Educational Leadership, William & Mary School of Education

"This publication is very timely. As I read the book, I was able to visualize how I would use it to provide professional development for my leadership team. The book called many of my actions into question, which has already reshaped my thinking as a leader. I would recommend this publication to school and district leaders."

—**Audrey White-Garner,** Elementary Principal, Richland School District One

"This playbook helps leaders break down complicated scenarios into manageable next steps. The exercises felt relevant to help me work through a leadership challenge, and determine the next right step, without taking an overwhelming amount of effort or time. This playbook would be beneficial for both novice and veteran leaders."

—**Jennifer Douglas,** Principal, Voris CLC, Akron Public Schools

HƎW
LEADERSHIP WORKS

Cathy Lassiter | Douglas Fisher
Nancy Frey | Dominique Smith

HOW
LEADERSHIP WORKS

a playbook
for Instructional Leaders

CORWIN
Fisher & Frey

FOR INFORMATION:

Corwin
A SAGE Company
2455 Teller Road
Thousand Oaks, California 91320
(800) 233-9936
www.corwin.com

SAGE Publications Ltd.
1 Oliver's Yard
55 City Road
London EC1Y 1SP
United Kingdom

SAGE Publications India Pvt. Ltd.
B 1/I 1 Mohan Cooperative Industrial Area
Mathura Road, New Delhi 110 044
India

SAGE Publications Asia-Pacific Pte. Ltd.
18 Cross Street #10-10/11/12
China Square Central
Singapore 048423

President: Mike Soules
Vice President and Editorial
  Director: Monica Eckman
Director and Publisher,
  Corwin Classroom: Lisa Luedeke
Senior Content Development
  Manager: Julie Nemer
Content Development Editor: Sharon Wu
Associate Content Development
  Editor: Sarah Ross
Editorial Assistant: Nancy Chung
Production Editor: Melanie Birdsall
Copy Editor: Lana Arndt
Typesetter: C&M Digitals (P) Ltd.
Proofreader: Sally Jaskold
Cover Designer: Rose Storey
Marketing Manager: Kerry Garagliano

Copyright © 2022 by Corwin Press, Inc.

All rights reserved. Except as permitted by U.S. copyright law, no part of this work may be reproduced or distributed in any form or by any means, or stored in a database or retrieval system, without permission in writing from the publisher.

When forms and sample documents appearing in this work are intended for reproduction, they will be marked as such. Reproduction of their use is authorized for educational use by educators, local school sites, and/or noncommercial or nonprofit entities that have purchased the book.

All third-party trademarks referenced or depicted herein are included solely for the purpose of illustration and are the property of their respective owners. Reference to these trademarks in no way indicates any relationship with, or endorsement by, the trademark owner.

Sketchnotes by Taryl Hansen

Printed in the United States of America

Library of Congress Cataloging-in-Publication Data

Names: Lassiter, Cathy J., author. | Fisher, Douglas, author. | Frey, Nancy, author. | Smith, Dominique, author.

Title: How leadership works : a playbook for instructional leaders / Cathy J. Lassiter, Douglas Fisher, Nancy Frey, Dominique B. Smith.

Description: Thousand Oaks, California : Corwin, [2022] | Includes bibliographical references and index.

Identifiers: LCCN 2021060092 | ISBN 9781071871058 (Spiral Bound) | ISBN 9781071877203 (ePub) | ISBN 9781071877197 (ePub) | ISBN 9781071877180 (PDF)

Subjects: LCSH: Educational leadership—United States. | School improvement programs—United States. | Teacher-principal relationships—United States. | Professional learning communities—United States.

Classification: LCC LB2822.82 .L39 2022 | DDC 371.2/011—dc23/eng/20220124

LC record available at https://lccn.loc.gov/2021060092

This book is printed on acid-free paper.

22 23 24 25 26 10 9 8 7 6 5 4 3

DISCLAIMER: This book may direct you to access third-party content via web links, QR codes, or other scannable technologies, which are provided for your reference by the author(s). Corwin makes no guarantee that such third-party content will be available for your use and encourages you to review the terms and conditions of such third-party content. Corwin takes no responsibility and assumes no liability for your use of any third-party content, nor does Corwin approve, sponsor, endorse, verify, or certify such third-party content.

Contents

Visit the companion website at
resources.corwin.com/howleadershipworks
for downloadable resources, tools, and guides.

Acknowledgments

Corwin gratefully acknowledges the contributions of the following reviewers:

Jennifer Douglas
Principal
Akron Public Schools
Uniontown, OH

Shannon Jackson
Executive Director of Teaching and Learning
Knox County Schools
Knoxville, TN

Kendra Washington-Bass
Educator, Leadership Development
Gwinnett County Public Schools
Grayson, GA

Audrey White-Garner
Elementary Principal
Richland School District One
Columbia, SC

Introduction

Exploring Leadership

Administrators and teacher-leaders face a number of tasks, ranging from lunchtime supervision to budget and discipline of students, all essential to keep a school operating. Unfortunately, for many educational leaders, pressing responsibilities related to school operations take precedent and interfere with their ability to serve as instructional leaders at the same time. Consequentially, educational leaders are prevented from spending time observing classroom instruction and talking to teachers about their professional practices that impact student learning.

Getting leaders into classrooms is important if school improvement efforts are to flourish. While necessary, spending time in classrooms and providing feedback is not sufficient to create lasting change. Lasting change requires an agreement on quality so that the leader and the teacher can have a productive conversation about the impact the instructional moves have on learning. We will return to this point later, but our experiences with school improvement efforts suggest that reaching agreements on quality are crucial if professional development efforts and administrative or peer feedback are to be effective.

School improvement efforts suggest that reaching agreements on quality are crucial if professional development efforts and administrative or peer feedback are to be effective.

As an example, think back to a conversation you've had with a teacher following a classroom observation. Say, for example, that you just returned from a conference that validated and extended your understanding of the importance of building on students' background knowledge. As part of the observation, you notice several opportunities that the teacher missed to build and activate background knowledge. The conversation you have might go something like this:

Leader: How do you think the lesson went?

Teacher: Great, I thought that my students were all engaged.

Leader: Yes, true, they all seemed interested in the topic. Did you think about what they might already know about the topic? Or what they might not know about it?

Teacher: No, not really. I think that they learned a lot from the experience. Did you hear them talking with each other?

Leader: Yes, they were talking and asking good questions. But what did they already know?

Teacher: I'm not sure. But I will bet that they do well on the assessment.

Leader: Did you think about making connections between their background knowledge and the topic at hand? Could it be that some of the students already knew this before the lesson?

Teacher: Sure, but that's what happens in every lesson. Some know it already, some get it, and others need more teaching.

Leader: I think it would be useful to tap into students' background knowledge and then build on that with students.

Teacher: Yeah, maybe. I really liked the summaries they wrote at the end. You didn't get to see that part, but I can show you want they wrote. See . . .

This conversation is not really getting anywhere because the two people have a different understanding of quality, at least in terms of the topic of background knowledge. As a result, the teacher is immune to the feedback being provided and is not likely to change because of the experience. For this reason, we think that quality is really priority one. Reaching agreements on quality provides a baseline from which a meaningful conversation can be had and changes can be addressed.

Now, imagine a school in which agreements about quality have been reached. There have been discussions about evidence-based practices that are likely to impact learning. The instructional leaders and teachers share definitions, allowing much more productive conversations between them. When there are agreements about quality, new initiatives are more likely to be implemented and thrive. When there are agreements about quality, educators (teachers and leaders) are more likely to abandon or de-implement practices that are not working. Leaders lead these instructional conversations and ensure that agreements about quality are the starting place and that teachers are supported in making change.

EXPLORING LEADERSHIP

Kevin Kruse (2013), author of *Great Leaders Have No Rules* (2019), asks a provocative question in his *Forbes* magazine article: What is leadership, anyway? He starts with what leadership is *not*:

➡ Leadership has nothing to do with seniority or one's position in the hierarchy of a company.

➡ Leadership has nothing to do with titles.

➡ Leadership has nothing to do with personal attributes.

➡ Leadership isn't management.

Instead, Kruse (2013) suggests that "leadership is a process of social influence, which maximizes the efforts of others, toward the achievement of a goal." Furthermore, he provides several key elements of this definition:

➡ Leadership stems from *social* influence, not authority or power.

➡ Leadership requires others, and that implies they don't need to be "direct reports."

➡ Leadership does not require certain attributes or even a title; there are many styles and many paths to effective leadership.

➡ It includes *a goal*, not influence with no intended outcome.

Is that how you see yourself? We hope so. Just think about how great schools would be if every leader exercised their social influence to create change. Just think how great schools would be if leaders were able to maximize the efforts of others. And just think how great schools would be if they worked toward a valued goal. We believe that these are within our reach and that this playbook will help you accomplish this leadership goal.

This playbook focuses on teaching and learning. Of course, there are other aspects of the work that site-based and central office leaders do, ranging from human resources to facilities management to lunch supervision. Although these operational aspects are important, leaders must attend to the instructional program if their schools and districts are going to deliver on the promise of equity and ensure excellence for all. Thus, as indicated by the book's subtitle, it's for people interested in instructional leadership. Moreover, we believe that every leader within the school system should understand the instructional focus and initiatives designed to support learning.

You will notice that we often include effect sizes to support our recommendations. To do so, we draw on the research by John Hattie. He has assembled the largest collection of meta-analyses about education—the Visible Learning® research collection. Through Corwin, he has made this research available at www.visiblelearningmetax.com to the public. A meta-analysis is a systematic review of research on a given topic. Using a statistical tool and reviewing the various studies, an effect size can be generated. This number tells us how powerful a given influence is in ensuring learning. Actions that we take with low effect sizes are not likely to ensure a lot of learning, whereas actions with higher effect sizes are more likely to ensure learning occurs.

The average of all the influences on learning collected to date is 0.40. Thus, anything above 0.40 is an above-average influence, and anything below 0.40 is below the average. That's not to say that we stop doing everything below 0.40. For example, counseling services have an effect size of 0.33, which is slightly below average in terms of impact on learning. However, you probably recognize that there are other reasons for providing counseling services. Whole school improvement efforts also have an effect size of 0.33, again slightly below the average. Does that mean we give up on whole school change, or do we recognize that many of our efforts to improve learning are not fully implemented? In fact, the last section of this book focuses on leading change, as well as implementation and de-implementation efforts. If we all get really good at this, the effect size for whole school improvement efforts should increase.

Let's take a look at two different effect sizes that involve leaders and our influence on decisions. The first is grade-level retention, which is failing and repeating a grade. We can see that the effect size on the barometer is *minus* 0.32. Note that it is in the reverse area, meaning that students actually learn less when they are retained. Although this is a team decision, leadership matters.

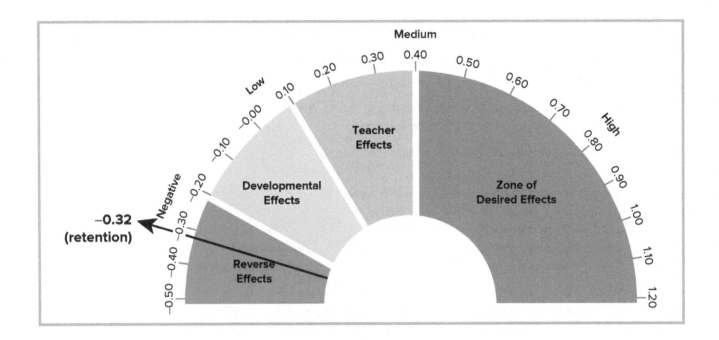

What might be the impact of providing quality intervention services rather than retaining a student? The barometer below holds the answer: an effect size of 1.09. Note that it falls well into the zone of desired effects. Armed with this information, leaders work to establish and maintain strong intervention efforts and work to avoid grade-level retention.

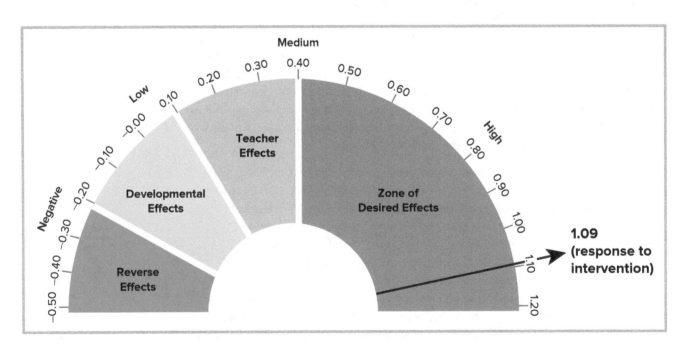

Importantly, Visible Learning is more than a list of effect sizes. Having analyzed the ways in which learning is impacted, Hattie has developed mindframes, or dispositions, that are based on the evidence collected. Mindframes describe the way we make decisions. There are mindframes for parents, students, teachers, and leaders. In Module 1, we explore the leader mindframes. Following this investigation, **Part I focuses on leading teaching.** A few teaching practices are discussed, such as teacher clarity and student engagement in learning, as well as the need to support teachers in delivering quality instructional experiences. Having said that, it's important that we do not spend all our time focused on teaching. We need to attend to the *impact* of that teaching: the learning. However, some approaches to teaching are much more likely than others to ensure that students gain a year's worth of learning for the year that they are in school, for example, using learning intentions and success criteria. You'll notice we model this practice at the start of each module in this book. As we will discuss in Module 9, both practices are well above average in terms of their impact on learning. Thus, we conclude Part I with tools to document the impact that teachers and teaching have on learners and learning.

In Part II, we focus on leading learning. In this section, we explore school culture, professional learning communities as a pathway to building collective teacher efficacy, and the value of feedback from teachers to students, from students to teachers, from teachers to leaders, and from leaders to teachers.

In Part III, we focus on applying the principles of change, conducting an initiative inventory, and focusing on implementation of initiatives, as well as the ways in which we can de-implement things that are not working.

Importantly, each module will reference the related mindframes as we build on the content discussed in the preceding modules.

Remember Kruse's definition that "leadership is a process of social influence, which maximizes the efforts of others, toward the achievement of a goal"? Your social influence can be powerful. With that comes great responsibility, and it requires that you understand the

- Evidence behind the initiatives you recommend
- Ways in which change occurs
- Goals you want to accomplish
- Impact you want to have
- Actions you are willing to take to support your team

We believe that veteran school leaders can deepen their knowledge and refine their leadership skills by engaging in the exercises and content in this playbook. Furthermore, we recommend that new and aspiring instructional leaders interact with this content to guide and frame priorities and practices that will result in greater impact on instruction. Finally, we see an important role for central office leaders in this work. Each of the modules can be used to support the learning of all staff engaged in instructional leadership. Therefore, administrators in professional development, school improvement, federal programs, curriculum and instruction, and principal supervision can enrich and expand their capacities to strengthen instructional leadership throughout the district by using this book.

And just like mathematics, art, reading, yoga, or most anything else, we can all learn to be great leaders. We are lucky to have you leading the work.

1

MINDFRAMES FOR LEADERS

LEARNING INTENTIONS

- I am learning about 10 leadership mindframes.
- I am learning to leverage the leadership mindframes to strengthen my skills and evaluate my impact.

SUCCESS CRITERIA

- I can explain the intent of the impact, change and challenge, and learning focus of the mindframes.
- I can analyze leadership practices for each mindframe and develop my own practices.
- I can assess my current mindframes and identify strengths and gaps.
- I can create a plan to intentionally develop the mindframes I need to lead instruction.

All schools deserve great leaders, not by chance, but by design. Schools with great leaders are better places for learning, and this is where students actually learn more. Furthermore, schools with great leaders have less turnover than schools with less effective leaders (well, some schools have higher turnover because the leader provides opportunities and supports others to become leaders). Teachers are happier at work and report higher job satisfaction where effective leaders lead. Finally, schools with great leaders are places that the community is proud of, and families are pleased that their children attend such schools.

Great school leadership cannot be left to chance. There are specific actions that leaders can take, as well as dispositions that we can adopt, to ensure that the schools we are responsible for are great places for learning, for both students and educators. Before focusing on the skills and strategies that are useful for great leaders, we will share several mindframes, or dispositions and habits, that are useful.

Hattie and Smith (2020) define the mindframes as a set of necessary dispositions or habits of mind that drive the performance of leaders. In other words, leaders' beliefs and values, their mindframes, determine their practices and ways of engaging with students, teachers, and parents. These useful ways of thinking and acting are captured in a total of 10 mindframes. They help site-based and central-office leaders focus their thinking and engage in self-reflection to strengthen their leadership practices and improve the learning lives of students and teachers.

A LEADER'S CHALLENGE

Tim is the principal of an elementary school where students come from homes in communities struggling to provide the basics of modern life, such as Internet access, healthy food sources, and quality recreational facilities. As the coronavirus pandemic changed the schooling format, Tim thought about the love, support, and services students might miss. He was also gravely concerned about the well-being of his teachers, as they were isolated from their colleagues, families, friends, and everyday activities. Although he was consumed by the many state mandates, ever-changing district plans, and his own ability to lead through the crisis, Tim was able to take some time to consider how his thinking was impacting his actions and the degree to which they would further impact his staff and students. Tim thought to himself, "What messages do I want our staff and families to hear and see from me that will help move us together through this crisis?" He determined the most important messages to communicate, including

➡ Children and their families need support, love, and grace.

➡ The most important thing is health, safety, and well-being.

➡ We will learn what we need to know about distance learning by supporting each other and making mistakes.

➡ We will roll with the punches, be flexible, and keep our students at the forefront of our decisions.

He then collaborated with his leadership team and developed an action plan that would clearly communicate a commitment to these ideas. He instituted a weekly virtual coffee time with the principal for staff to connect, get the latest updates, share worries and concerns, and have some fun. Furthermore, he established a weekly family news brief and posted it online. He then searched for and provided quality professional learning to help all educators, including himself, learn about the tools, platforms, and best practices for distance learning. Importantly, he responded to the many changes in plans that rolled in from the district office. He remained calm and presented the changes to staff with a can-do spirit and confidence that they would get through it together. He took care of students and their families by providing food pick-ups, lessons in technology, and phone calls to check in with empathy and grace. Tim and staff also visited students' homes, leaving goodie bags filled with school supplies, books, and snacks, as well as important information about support services and learning programs.

Over time, as the format of school continues to change, Tim continues to assess his mindframes and strives to serve as a model during confusing and uncertain times. This is Tim's leadership challenge.

PAUSE AND PONDER

Which of Tim's leadership behaviors indicate that he is an effective leader?

_____

_____

_____

_____

_____

_____

_____

_____

_____

_____

❊ A Work in Progress

SELF-ASSESS YOUR INTENTIONALITY

How intentional are you? For each of the following statements, indicate the extent to which it is part of your practice:

	Rarely	Sometimes	Always
I consider my mindframes before embarking on a change project with my staff.			
I am mindful of how my actions and behavior impact how the staff are thinking and acting.			
I determine the impact I wish to have with staff and students before I act.			
I intentionally model the behaviors and actions I hope to see in staff.			
I seek evidence to inform my thinking and leading.			
I am more proactive than reactive when making decisions.			
I am driven by a set of leadership mindframes that impact my leadership actions.			

Which rating (rarely, sometimes, or always) did you select most often?

What can you infer from your ratings regarding how well you are currently leading instructional initiatives?

Based on your ratings and inferences, what are some potential starting points for you to lead instructional improvement?

TEN LEADERSHIP MINDFRAMES

According to Hattie and Zierer (2018), "The way we think about the impact of what we do is more important than what we do." They offer 10 mindframes that encourage teachers and leaders to be more intentional about the ways we think about our impact on learners and learning. These mindframes drive how we do our work in very specific ways. For leaders, the mindframes inform how we lead professional learning, give feedback, coach improvement, and hire and support quality teachers. The mindframes "focus on self-regulation—or the ability to control and direct one's behavior, emotions, and thoughts" (Fisher et al., 2021a, p. 92).

"The way we think about the impact of what we do is more important than what we do" (Hattie & Zierer, 2018).

The 10 mindframes for leaders listed below, introduced by Hattie and Smith (2020), were divided into the following three main categories:

➡ Impact mindframes

➡ Change and challenge mindframes

➡ Learning focus mindframes

We have retained these categories and made slight adaptations to keep the focus on instructional leadership. The mindframes and three categories are listed below.

MINDFRAMES FOR EFFECTIVE LEADERSHIP

Impact Mindframes

1. I am an evaluator of my impact on teacher and student learning.
2. I see evidence and data as informing my impact and next steps.
3. I collaborate with peers, teachers, students, and families about my conceptions of progress and my impact.

Change and Challenge Mindframes

4. I am a change agent, and I believe my role is to improve the learning lives of teachers and students.
5. I embrace challenge, and I support teachers and students in doing the same, not just doing our best.

Learning Focus Mindframes

6. I foster a culture of feedback where teachers, students, and leaders seek, give, receive, and act on feedback.
7. I engage as much in dialogue as in monologue.
8. I explicitly inform teachers and students what successful impact looks like from the outset.
9. I build relationships and trust to make it safe to make mistakes and learn from others.
10. I focus on learning and contribute to a shared language of learning.

Source: Hattie & Smith (2020).

We provide a narrative description of each of the 10 mindframes and a brief list of leadership practices that are examples of the mindframe in action. The mindframes and associated leadership practices can serve as guideposts for leaders to engage effectively in the three main areas of instructional leadership that follow in Parts I–III of this playbook. These parts focus on leading teaching, leading learning, and leading change.

Hattie tells us that Mindframe 1, "I am an evaluator of my impact," is the most important of all, as it serves as an umbrella for the remaining nine mindframes.

Impact Mindframes

Mindframe 1: I am an evaluator of my impact on teacher and student learning.

This mindframe is the essence of effective leadership. It means that leaders must be as deliberate about measuring the impact of leadership decisions and practices as they are in planning actions and practices. It is one thing to thoughtfully plan and implement ideas, and quite another to focus on the impact of the decisions and actions on the people affected by them. Evaluators of impact actively look for, measure, and respond to the impact their decisions have on learning, culture, efficacy, and equity.

MINDFRAME 1: LEADERSHIP PRACTICES

- Survey staff for successes and challenges with a new instructional practice.

- Walk the halls and check in with staff by doing "one-legged interviews" (i.e., short informal conversations that focus on how a change or practice is going. The name comes from the advice that the length of the interview corresponds to the amount of time you can stand on one leg).

- Monitor student benchmark data to capture trend lines tied to instructional practices.

- Routinely survey all stakeholders informally and formally on progress of new practices or changes recently implemented. Act on the feedback to improve support for deep implementation.

Mindframe 2: I see evidence and data as informing my impact and next steps.

Mindframe 2 requires leaders to engage in a courageous pursuit of evidence of impact and an open-minded reflection to drive next steps. Too often most of our energy and effort is exerted at the front end of a change initiative, rather than throughout the initiative. Unfortunately, after the initiative roll-out, we cannot assume that everyone affected understands what to do. This is what leads to so many failed initiatives. If you really want to know your impact, look deeply and listen for it, and prepare to make adjustments to your practices along the way.

MINDFRAME 2: LEADERSHIP PRACTICES

- Conduct learning walks to collect evidence on the deep implementation of new instructional practices and plan professional learning sessions to close teachers' gaps in understanding.

- Visit grade level or department meetings and professional learning community sessions to determine from teachers what support has helped them and what support has not been helpful. Adjust leadership practices accordingly to better support staff.

- Host regular talks with students about what is and is not working in their classrooms, and what changes they believe would improve their learning. Work with staff to authentically review and act on this feedback.

Mindframe 3: I collaborate with peers, teachers, students, and families about my conceptions of progress and my impact.

Building a shared understanding and commitment to a change vision is essential for progress and impact. Rarely, if ever, is a leader's desired impact achieved quickly. Therefore, collaboration regarding what incremental success might look like and how to measure impact over time is necessary. Leaders possessing this mindframe plan their communications with stakeholder groups and develop clarity of thought about what progress looks like. Then, leaders communicate in a way that provides stakeholders with clarity on the *why*, *what*, and *how* of the work ahead.

MINDFRAME 3: LEADERSHIP PRACTICES

- Meet with the school leadership team before, during, and after the change work gets underway to share your conceptions of progress and seek input from the team to refine and edit your conceptions based on their thoughts.

- Hold coffee chats or small focus group talks with families to discuss the work, the desired impact of the work, and the feedback you will seek to keep the work on track.

- Review student benchmark data with teachers and determine next steps for success. Share your conceptions of what progress looks like and the support you are prepared to provide to make steady progress to achieve the desired impact.

 A Work in Progress

IMPACT MINDFRAMES

Previously, we shared 10 examples of leadership practices linked to the impact mindframes. In the chart that follows, on the left, add your current practices that align to the impact mindframes. On the right, record practices you are thinking about undertaking to strengthen your leadership for impact.

Mindframes 1–3: Current Practices That Align	Practices I Am Considering
1.	
2.	
3.	
4.	
5.	

Change and Challenge Mindframes

Mindframe 4: I am a change agent, and I believe my role is to improve the learning lives of teachers and students.

Change agents are design thinkers, envelope pushers, risk-takers, and creative problem solvers. Leaders who routinely ask themselves how they can make things better are most likely driven by this mindframe. The learning lives of teachers and students encompass how they learn in groups, how they learn from mistakes, how they use feedback, how they work as a team, how they practice new skills, and how they see themselves as learners. A leader has a significant influence on these aspects of school life. Change agents realize this and serve their schools as leaders who constantly review and refine their leadership to enhance the learning lives of staff and students.

Change agents are design thinkers, envelope pushers, risk-takers, and creative problem solvers.

MINDFRAME 4: LEADERSHIP PRACTICES

- Collect and use feedback from staff following professional learning experiences to improve the impact on building the staff capacity.

- Provide and model collaboration protocols for professional learning community plus (PLC+) meetings to keep teachers focused and productive during their team time.

- Monitor student learning outcomes and collaborate with teachers on what is working and what is not to plan refinements to the instructional program.

- Explicitly talk about what it means to be a learner and model the dispositions of a learner for staff and students.

Mindframe 5: I embrace challenge, and I support teachers and students in doing the same, not just doing our best.

An essential quality of leaders is a willingness to embrace and thrive on challenge. Leaders who embrace challenge recognize that meeting a challenge might be uncomfortable. It could be frustrating and maybe even exhausting, but the struggle is worth it if it results in better learning for teachers and/or students. As Doug says, "We are in an anti-struggle era" when it comes to classroom challenges. Teachers often protect students from productive struggle, frontload too much, or rescue students when they see signs of struggle, which robs them of the thrill of learning something that is both difficult and complex. Adults, teachers, and leaders improve outcomes when they embrace productive struggle. This may involve persevering in learning more effective teaching strategies, finding solutions to assist struggling learners, or working toward shared agreements with PLC+ members. Adults who embrace challenge and bounce back after disappointments are much more likely to experience success and satisfaction as educators.

From the leaders to the teachers and to the students, struggle should be normalized and viewed as an essential part of learning. Learning is supposed to be hard work, both for adults and students.

MINDFRAME 5: LEADERSHIP PRACTICES

- Normalize challenge and productive struggle among adults and students.

- Share appropriate personal examples of embracing a challenge and persisting through struggle.

- Share examples of embracing challenge in classrooms.

- Make embracing challenge a valued learner disposition for all learners.

 Working on the Work

TEXT RENDERING PROTOCOL

Re-read the descriptions of Mindframes 4 and 5. Choose a most significant sentence, phrase, and word for each mindframe and record them in the chart on the next page or highlight them in your book. Examine your choices, make inferences, and use the reflection question following the chart to consider your selections.

Mindframe 4: Change Agent	Mindframe 5: Embrace Challenge
Significant sentence	**Significant sentence**
Significant phrase	**Significant phrase**
Significant word	**Significant word**

What do your choices tell you about your current mindframes as related to being a change agent and embracing challenge?

_____

_____

_____

Learning Focus Mindframes

Mindframe 6: I foster a culture of feedback where teachers, students, and leaders seek, give, receive, and act on feedback.

The way humans improve at anything—whether it is golf, cooking, writing, or leading—comes from quality feedback followed by deliberate practice. Therefore, if schools are to benefit from this powerful influence, leaders must commit to creating a _culture_ of feedback. When there is such a culture, leaders and teachers explicitly teach learners what feedback is, why it is important, how to give feedback using success criteria, and how to respond to feedback once it is received. Leaders who embrace Mindframe 6 establish norms and routines to enable streams of feedback to flow freely to and from students, teachers, and leaders. This culture of feedback is built on a foundation of trust-, empathy-, and growth-producing relationships, which will be discussed in-depth in Mindframe 9.

MINDFRAME 6: LEADERSHIP PRACTICES

- Seek feedback from staff on the implementation of new practices. Analyze and share the feedback with them and the actions you will take to respond to it.

- Engage students in all classes in peer feedback based on success criteria as an integral part of the instructional program.

- Support teachers in collecting feedback from their students to improve the effectiveness of teaching practices.

Mindframe 7: I engage as much in dialogue as in monologue.

Leaders with this mindframe understand that talking *with* people is more effective than talking *at* people. Dialogue enables us to learn new ideas, consider various perspectives, find different solutions to problems, and engage others in meaningful work. Dialogue involves active listening, questioning to understand, and responding thoughtfully and honoring the views of many. Dialogue is growth producing. Monologue, although necessary at times, is simply a means to direct people to certain tasks or provide them with information. Monologue is rarely growth producing for those involved.

MINDFRAME 7: LEADERSHIP PRACTICES

- Model dialogue as a value by thoughtfully listening, questioning, and responding to all stakeholders.

- Honor ideas developed through dialogue by implementing them.

- Encourage and support teachers in doing the same with their students.

- Share/teach specific conversation stems and sentence starters for teachers to use to spur quality class dialogue (adults could use these, too!).

Mindframe 8: I explicitly inform teachers and students what successful impact looks like from the outset.

According to Buckingham (2016), "Clarity is the antidote to anxiety." Teachers, as well as students, should be able to confidently respond to the following three questions related to their learning:

➡ What am I learning?

➡ Why am I learning this?

➡ How will I know that I learned it?

This clarity relies on teachers knowing at the start of the year what successful impact looks like in their classroom. For students, it means knowing what success looks like at the start of each unit and lesson: It is the leader's responsibility to communicate and to act with clarity toward shared goals.

MINDFRAME 8: LEADERSHIP PRACTICES

- Communicate, communicate, and communicate again the expectations and desired impact to ensure a shared understanding of goals and expected impact.

- Collaboratively develop a set of success criteria for expected outcomes and base feedback on the criteria.

- Seek feedback from teachers on support they will need to reach the expected outcomes. What do they need to learn? How can leaders support them? What resources would be helpful?

- Monitor results and the effectiveness of supports along the way.

Mindframe 9: I build relationships and trust to make it safe to make mistakes and learn from others.

Mindframe 9 is the critical foundation that allows learning to occur. When human beings feel a sense of belonging at work, when they experience relational trust from their leaders and colleagues, and when they are able to learn from mistakes and each other, deep learning and growth are likely to happen. When these elements are not part of the school culture, deep learning is unlikely.

MINDFRAME 9: LEADERSHIP PRACTICES

- Administer a survey to determine current levels of trust in the school and work with the leadership team to build a plan to improve trust among and with all colleagues.

- Implement team-building exercises at meetings and gatherings.

- Establish peer learning walks and debrief sessions to build efficacy.

- Support staff when learning something new and give grace during the learning period.

- Collect teacher perspectives regularly and respond with genuine interest.

Mindframe 10: I focus on learning and contribute to a shared language of learning.

When leaders focus on learning, they lead their teams in understanding how learning happens, they value teaching students how to be learners, they advocate for certain learner dispositions that all learners in their school can activate when needed, and they reinforce the concept that productive struggle and challenge are essential for successful learning. In principle, they create a learning culture where the learning process and learner dispositions are commonplace in conversations, lessons, data discussions, parent meetings, and all other aspects of school life. Leaders driven by this mindframe prioritize learning-focused work with teachers and spend significant time doing it.

MINDFRAME 10: LEADERSHIP PRACTICES

- Create a video diary of students' current conceptions of learning by asking students, "What makes a good learner?" Record their answers and analyze their responses with the staff. How many students responded with behavior- or compliance-based answers such as "listen to the teacher," "don't disrupt others," or "do your work"? How many students responded with qualities of a learner such as "be persistent," "ask questions," "collaborate," "embrace a challenge," and so forth?

- Work with the staff to create a profile of an ideal learner for your school.

- Conduct research on how learners learn and teach that process to staff and students.

- Routinely talk with staff and parents about learning—how learning happens, what good learners do, and how to learn from mistakes.

 A Work in Progress

LEARNING FOCUS MINDFRAMES, MINDFRAMES 6–10

In this module, we shared 20 examples of leadership practices for the learning focus mindframes. In the chart that follows, on the left, list your current practices that align to the learning mindframes. On the opposite side, record practices you consider undertaking to strengthen your leadership for impact.

Mindframes 6–10: Current Practices That Align	Practices I Am Considering
1.	
2.	
3.	
4.	
5.	

EFFECTIVE LEADERSHIP MINDFRAMES, MINDFRAMES 1–10

Reflect on your responses in previous exercises and your notes on the learning focus mindframes leading to this point. For each of the mindframes that follow, mark whether your learning on this mindframe *affirmed* current thinking, *extended* your thinking by adding something new, or *challenged* your thinking by prompting you to consider changes to your current practices. This assessment will help you capture your experience with this content and then make decisions on what your next step might be in conquering a challenge you are facing now.

Mindframes for Instructional Leadership	Affirmed	Extended	Challenged
1. I am an evaluator of my impact on teacher and student learning.			
2. I see evidence and data as informing my impact and next steps.			
3. I collaborate with peers, teachers, students, and families about my conceptions of progress and my impact.			
4. I am a change agent, and I believe my role is to improve the learning lives of teachers and students.			
5. I embrace challenge, and I support teachers and students in doing the same, not just doing our best.			
6. I foster a culture of feedback where teachers, students, and leaders seek, give, receive, and act on feedback.			
7. I engage as much in dialogue as in monologue.			
8. I explicitly inform teachers and students what successful impact looks like from the outset.			
9. I build relationships and trust to make it safe to make mistakes and learn from others.			
10. I focus on learning and contribute to a shared language of learning.			

>>> Working on the Work

Think of an important challenge or change you are working on now. Record this challenge in the box and answer the questions that follow.

My leadership challenge is . . .

The mindframes I need for success on this challenge include:

To ensure success on my challenge or change, I need to intentionally develop mindframes:

ALL IN A DAY'S WORK

Consider the questions below and complete the chart to capture your thinking about how to lead effectively with the 10 mindframes.

Which of your current practices align most strongly with the mindframes?

➡ Place these practices in the KEEP section of the chart.

Which of your current practices are not in alignment with any of the 10 mindframes?

➡ Place these practices in the STOP section of the chart.

What practices are you considering adding to strengthen your leadership aligned to the mindframes?

➡ Place these practices in the START section of the chart.

ACTIONS	PRACTICES BASED ON MY LEARNING IN THIS MODULE:
KEEP	I will continue to . . .
STOP	I will stop . . .
START	I will start . . .

CONCLUSION

In this module, you focused on the mindframes for effective leadership and were provided information and exercises to establish foundational knowledge that will enrich your reading of the remaining modules. To provide great instructional leadership for all schools, leaders must remain deliberate and unwavering in their quest to positively impact the learning lives of the students and the working lives of their teachers. The 10 mindframes serve as a guide and anchor for leaders to self-reflect and self-regulate toward more effective leadership.

Access resources, tools, and guides
for this module at the companion website:
resources.corwin.com/howleadershipworks

THE WORK AHEAD LEADING TEACHING

1

Remember those first-day jitters? The excitement and anticipation of a new class of students? Remember learning all those names and interests? And planning learning experiences designed to engage learners in meaningful tasks? And collecting evidence of student learning, realizing you had an impact? We have so many fond memories of our teaching experiences.

Now, our roles have changed. We have widened our sphere of influence. Rather than being responsible for a class of 30, we are responsible for 300 or 3,000 or 30,000 or 100,000+ students. However, teaching is still a significant part of our job. The learners in front of us may be adults, but we nonetheless need to design or ensure amazing learning experiences for them. As their leaders, we must demonstrate our instructional leadership and ensure that quality experiences are occurring in every classroom. And we help teachers and other educators understand that they have an impact on learning.

This part focuses on teaching, although we don't dive into many specific instructional strategies. Yes, there are several tools teachers can use to impact learning, such as

- Jigsaw, with an effect size of 1.20

- Reciprocal teaching, with an effect size of 0.74

- Direct instruction, with an effect size of 0.59

- Classroom discussion, with an effect size of 0.82

However, there is not just one way to teach or one strategy that will work for all students. In fact, we argued that teachers should not hold any strategy in higher esteem than student learning. In other words, change the strategy if students are not learning. Instead of telling teachers how to teach, leaders should ensure that teachers have important conversations about the tools they use and the impact their choices have on learning.

In this part, we focus on

- Demonstrating instructional leadership (Module 2)

- Supporting teacher clarity and promoting student engagement (Module 3)

- Investigating the impact of teaching (Module 4)

2

DEMONSTRATE INSTRUCTIONAL LEADERSHIP

LEARNING INTENTIONS

- I am learning about specific practices of effective instructional leaders.
- I am exploring ways to incorporate instructional leadership practices into my work.

SUCCESS CRITERIA

- I can make the connection between instructional leadership and the leader mindframes.
- I can differentiate between transformational and instructional leadership.
- I can explain the most powerful practices of instructional leadership.
- I can engage in meaningful and productive post-observation dialogue with teachers.
- I can recognize the practices and pitfalls of building relational trust.
- I can self-regulate to build self-efficacy for strong instructional leadership.

Following years of widespread assumptions that school leaders had limited impact on student learning, the past 20 years of research on leadership in schools clearly demonstrate principals' influence. The Wallace Foundation's report (Grissom et al., 2021), *How Principals Affect Students and Schools*, documents the impact of school principals on student learning, noting that this influence may not have been stated strongly enough in previous reports. Given that the impacts of principals are seen largely through their effects on teachers, including how they hire, develop, support, and retain talented teaching staff, as well as create cultures in which teachers can do their best work, how principals approach leading their schools directly affects school outcomes. As Manna (2015) reminds, leaders can be both magnifiers and multipliers of effective instruction.

When it comes to school improvement, the evidence suggests that principal effectiveness may be more important than individual teacher effectiveness. Consider that the average elementary classroom has 21 students; thus, an effective teacher impacts 21 students. However, the average size of an elementary school is 483, meaning an effective school principal impacts 483 students. How to leverage this impact through effective instructional leadership is the focus of this module. Unfortunately, the promise of this impact has yet to be realized as the effect size of principals is 0.34. We'll explain why later in this module.

A LEADER'S CHALLENGE

Jermaine is the principal of a large suburban high school that is well-funded by the community and enjoys a good reputation among parents. The school's athletic program is one of the best in the district, and the students have access to quality arts programs as well. Student achievement results are stable, just above the state average. Graduates generally go on to attend state universities, and some attend Ivy Leagues. About 20% of the students enroll in career and technical programs, join the military, and/or access post-secondary careers and community colleges. Jermaine often reminds the staff and students about the school's vision and mission: growing leaders for the future!

Jermaine frequently visits classrooms to check in with staff and say hello to students. He supports the teachers in trying new things and trusts them to deliver quality instruction every day. He encourages teachers to work together and share best practices; however, the master schedule does not allow time for this collaborative work. The teachers, students, and parents support Jermaine, and his stakeholder survey data are generally positive.

Jermaine does not subscribe to the notion that the district office knows what is best for his students, so he frequently shelters teachers from the practices, directives, mandates, and recommendations that are issued. This often leads to conversations with his supervisor about his support of district initiatives. The district leadership expects principals to not only visit classrooms, but to also effectively observe instruction, meet with teachers, and coach for improvement. They also expect school leaders to foster teacher collaboration and provide time for team learning. Finally, they expect that teachers and leaders will evaluate their impact on learning. These have all been points of discussion between Jermaine and his supervisor. However, in Jermaine's way of thinking, as long as parents and students are happy, and the school demonstrates good enough performance on state assessments, he is doing his job well. This difference in opinion is Jermaine's leadership challenge.

PAUSE AND PONDER

How might Jermaine balance the expectations from the district while ensuring that teachers are not overwhelmed? Do you think the expectations from central office to visit classrooms and observe instruction are reasonable? Is performance just above the state average acceptable?

_____

_____

_____

_____

_____

_____

_____

_____

_____

_____

✳ A Work in Progress

TRANSFORMATIONAL AND INSTRUCTIONAL LEADERS

The chart that follows contains a list of practices of both transformational and instructional leaders. Rank order these practices from where you spend the most time to the least amount of time. A rank of 1 will indicate the practice where you spend the most time, and a rank of 10 will indicate the practice on which you spend the least amount of time. Suggestion: Read all the statements first, then go back and complete the ranking.

Rank	Leadership Practice
	1. Visiting classes to check in on teachers and students
	2. Implementing the teacher evaluation process to ensure student learning
	3. Meeting with the leadership team to ensure teachers have what they need
	4. Observing instruction for practices that are known to improve learning

(Continued)

(Continued)

Rank	Leadership Practice
	5. Communicating the vision and mission to stakeholders
	6. Participating in professional learning communities plus meetings where teachers analyze data and plan lessons to meet student learning needs
	7. Recognizing teacher accomplishments
	8. Leading, organizing, and participating in professional learning with teachers
	9. Keeping teachers informed on progress toward school goals
	10. Providing teachers meaningful feedback for instructional improvement and growth in student learning

List the numbers of the items that you gave top rankings (i.e., 1, 2, and 3).

_____

_____

_____

List the numbers of the items that you ranked at the bottom (i.e., 8, 9, and 10).

_____

_____

_____

The odd numbers represent practices of *transformational leaders,* and the even numbers are practices of *instructional leaders*. Are you spending your time on the practices that research shows have the greatest impact on student learning?

_____

_____

_____

How can you re-purpose some of the time you spend outside of instructional leadership and apply it to instructional leadership practices?

_____

_____

_____

REACHING CLARITY ON INSTRUCTIONAL LEADERSHIP

Our efforts in transformational leadership and our efforts to improve instructional experiences create different learning outcomes. You may be thinking that transforming schools requires, in part, improvements in instructional experiences. That's true. But these contrasting leadership practices require different actions and areas of focus for leaders. Transformational leadership thus involves setting the vision and mission for the school, energizing teachers, filtering demands of their time from outside sources, and supporting teacher autonomy in the classroom. In short, transformational leaders focus on teachers.

Conversely, instructional leaders spend much more time in classrooms, observing and engaging in instruction, building collective trust to enable learning by mistake-making, fostering collegiality via professional learning communities, supporting peer learning walks and peer coaching, providing growth-oriented feedback and instructional coaching, and providing quality professional development focused on improving the learning lives of both staff and students. Instructional leaders seek to evaluate their impact on learning, inform teachers on what successful impact looks like, and set appropriate levels of challenge for both staff and students. In short, instructional leaders focus on students and all aspects that influence their learning.

Instructional leaders focus on students and all aspects that influence their learning.

Nearly 80% of survey respondents indicated that they most closely identified with the characteristics of transformational leadership over instructional leadership (Marks, 2013). In a meta-analysis of leadership styles, Robinson et al. (2008) noted that the effect size for transformational leaders was 0.11. That's pretty minimal. The overall effect size for instructional leaders was 0.42. That's a noteworthy difference and explains why principals have a slightly below-average impact on learning at 0.34: Too many are focused on transformational leadership. This is not to say that transformational leadership lacks any positive impact. And teachers do need to be supported in their work. But Hattie (2015, p. 38) noted the following influences of leaders that are well above average. This is the work that leaders need to be doing.

➡ Leaders who believe their major role is to evaluate their impact (effect size = 0.91)

➡ Leaders who get everyone in the school working together to know and evaluate their impact (effect size = 0.91)

➡ Leaders who learn in an environment that privileges high-impact teaching and learning (effect size = 0.84)

➡ Leaders who are explicit with teachers and students about what success looks like (effect size = 0.77)

➡ Leaders who set appropriate levels of challenge and who never retreat to "just do your best" (effect size = 0.57)

SELF-EFFICACY FOR INSTRUCTIONAL LEADERSHIP

Some leaders recognize that they can lead the instructional focus of their schools, and others not so much. In other words, some leaders have strong efficacy in this aspect of their work. There are several practices that require strong self-efficacy to be effective in school leadership, including

➡ Developing goals and vision for the school

➡ Developing a collective culture

➡ Motivating teachers

➡ Conducting classroom observations

➡ Guiding teachers and creating a positive and safe learning environment for students

Evidence (e.g., Skaalvik, 2020) shows that principals with a low sense of self-efficacy to lead instruction actually avoid their instructional leadership duties. They may be doing so because they feel uncomfortable and unsuccessful or simply because they do not believe that they have time. These feelings of inadequacy add to their stress levels because they know instructional leadership is of great importance. When leaders feel inadequate in this area, their well-being and motivation suffer. Importantly, people generally avoid situations for which they have low mastery skills, and it may explain why some school leaders immerse themselves in managerial responsibilities.

So why does this matter to you? If you are finding that you are unable to focus on instructional leadership due to your engagement in other managerial duties, or you focus on transformational leadership practices, you may lack the confidence and self-efficacy to engage deeply in instructional leadership. It will take some soul searching on your part to determine if this is the root cause of not focusing on the duties and actions of instructional leaders.

 A Work in Progress

SELF-EFFICACY

To get started, read each of the statements below and check either *Yes* or *No* in response to *I am certain that I can . . .*

I am certain that I can . . .	Yes	No
1. Guide teachers on educational outcomes		
2. Observe teaching and provide meaningful feedback		
3. Develop clear instructional expectations for teachers		

I am certain that I can . . .	Yes	No
4. Lead professional learning on high-effect pedagogy		
5. Engage confidently in conversations about instructional quality		
6. Create enthusiasm among teachers for quality teaching and learning		
7. Develop a culture of collaboration for instructional improvement		
8. Establish structures and routines that build teacher efficacy		
9. Create a shared language of learning across the school community		
10. Support professional learning communities		
Total of *Yes* and *No* responses		

If you have three or more *No* responses, you may lack a strong sense of self-efficacy for instructional leadership. But this can change. You can strengthen your self-efficacy by taking charge of your development as an instructional leader. Consider reaching out to a trusted colleague known to be a strong instructional leader and learn from them. Work with a mentor who can coach you in instructional leadership. Seek professional learning opportunities to develop your skills as an instructional leader, access district resources to support your development, and become a reader of articles and books focused on instructional leadership. Finally, you must start engaging in the work and be willing to make and learn from mistakes to build your instructional leadership skills and confidence. As you study the remaining sections of this module, be mindful of your own sense of efficacy to do this work and target content that might address gaps in your skill bank.

Consider the following reflection questions for central office leaders charged with supporting the learning and development of school-based leaders:

- To what extent do you and/or your team intentionally address the self-efficacy of school leaders for instructional leadership?

- What learning opportunities might you provide to build the knowledge, skill, and personal confidence of school leaders to lead instruction in their schools?

WHAT DO STRONG INSTRUCTIONAL LEADERS DO?

The best available research tells us that the four most influential leadership practices to improve school outcomes happen when school leaders prioritize their time to interact with teachers around instructional topics. The four behaviors with the most impact are

1. Engaging in instructionally focused interactions with teachers

2. Building a productive school climate

3. Facilitating productive collaboration and professional learning communities

4. Managing personnel and resources strategically

Given that the principal's impact on learning is indirect and comes through teachers, it makes sense that the most important work of school leaders is ensuring that they have a talented teaching team that focuses on learning for all students. For students, teachers are critically important, but simultaneously, students learn more in schools with effective principals because all classrooms are led by quality teachers (Grissom et al., 2021). This is why *managing personnel and resources strategically* are so important to improving school outcomes.

Students learn more in schools with effective principals because all classrooms are led by quality teachers.

Number three, above, tells us that *facilitating productive collaboration and professional learning communities* is another of the four most influential leadership practices to improve school outcomes. Effective instructional leaders lead and participate in professional learning activities with teachers. They possess a deep knowledge of research-based pedagogical approaches, and they know how to teach and support the implementation of new practices in the classroom. As a teacher of teachers, principals can model strong teaching skills and effective use of engagement strategies that they hope to see in all classrooms. They might model the use of the school's focus strategies or "evergreen practices" to build credibility and demonstrate competence as an educator and instructional leader. When principals are not leading the learning, they secure quality professional learning conducted by others. They support, promote, and participate in the learning with teachers to demonstrate the importance of the learning, model professional learning for staff, and learn from staff about the potential challenges going forward. Instructional leaders recognize that a learning culture for all has a significant impact on the learning outcomes for students and, therefore, emphasizes learning as a core value.

The second leadership practice notes the importance of a *productive school climate*. In fact, school climate is one of the above-average influences on student learning. Every school we have ever been in has a feel to it; it's noticeable from the time you enter the building. In some places, school culture is left to chance, and in others, it is nurtured and developed. A healthy school culture includes trust, belonging, and respect, but also high expectations for learning and safety when it comes to making mistakes.

The first leadership practice tells us that *engaging in instructionally focused interactions with teachers* highly influences a school's outcomes. This is the foundation for engaging with teachers on instructional matters. However, to improve instruction, you must know instruction. Effective principals spend time in classrooms, looking formally and informally at instructional practices. They talk with students about what they are learning, why they are learning, and how they will know they are learning. They leave notes of appreciation and recognition of teachers' efforts on their desks before they leave. They enjoy follow-up conversations with teachers to discuss impact and next steps, and feedback is delivered via respectful conversations. Effective instructional leaders do not consider observing instruction a dreaded chore. Rather, they look forward to classroom visits and discussions with teachers. It's the joy of the job!

On the pages that follow, you will find a sample conversation protocol for having meaningful conversations with teachers about instruction following classroom observations. This process encourages dialogue over monologue, Mindframe 7, and leverages the best practices of listening, paraphrasing, and questioning for understanding to work with teachers on their next steps. The protocol is divided into three parts and contains examples to use in the conversations. As you read through each part, circle or tag steps in the protocol that you want to incorporate into your conversations. Or you can use the protocol as is to ensure meaningful dialogue about improving instruction.

A Work in Progress

PROTOCOL FOR COACHING INSTRUCTION

Part I: Welcome and Establish Goals for Session

Step	Conversation Details	Conversation Notes
1	**Opening** Be warm, genuine, and thank the teacher for taking time away from students to meet with you.	
2	**Teacher's Lesson Aim** Ask the teacher to explain the aim of the lesson you observed. LISTEN, and record the response to the right.	Teacher's lesson aim was . . .
3	**Teacher's Aim for the Conversation** Ask the teacher to share the aim for the conversation today. LISTEN, paraphrase, and question responses: For example, *So, you would like to explore effective ways to engage students in deeper thinking . . .* *Can you elaborate? Can you say more?*	Teacher's aim for the conversation . . .
4	**Principal's Aim for the Conversation** State your goal for the conversation. Acknowledge the teacher's aim and add your aim. For example, *That information is very helpful to me. I think we can explore ways to get the students more deeply into their learning.* *My goal for the conversation today is to highlight the effective pieces of your lesson, work with you on your goals and the goals of the school, and collaborate on options for next steps. Let's get started.*	

Part II: Determine Strengths, Challenges, and Opportunities for Growth

Step	Conversation Details	Conversation Notes
5	**Teacher Comment on What's Going Well** Ask the teacher what went well in the lesson and/or what has been going well overall in the classroom to get started. LISTEN and paraphrase/question what the teacher says.	What the teacher feels went well . . .

(Continued)

(Continued)

Step	Conversation Details	Conversation Notes
	For example, *It sounds like _____ has been a growing success in your lessons since the quarter began. Is that right?* *What do you attribute that to? What else do you feel went well? How do you know it went well?*	
6	**Principal Comments on What Went Well** Repeat what the teacher feels went well and say, *I appreciate that you feel _____ and _____ went well. I would like to add that I felt _____ went well too. Specifically, I saw _____. I heard _____. I observed students doing _____ and _____.*	
7	**Determine Challenges** Transition the conversation to reflection and areas for improvement to be determined collaboratively with the teacher. Ask the teacher to identify parts of the lesson that could be strengthened. For example, *Were there any parts of the lesson that you feel might have been more effective? What did you notice the students doing during this section of the lesson? What would you have liked to see from the students instead?* LISTEN, paraphrase, and question the teacher's responses, seeking to paraphrase and ask questions to ensure you understand the teacher's feelings about how the lesson went. For example, *So, you believe that the transitions from one part of the lesson to the next caused the students to become unfocused. Is that right?* *Can you think of an example of when that occurred? Why is this important to you during the lesson?*	What the teacher feels was a challenge . . .
8	**Lead Reflection to Address Challenges** Lead an exploration about how to address the teacher's areas for improvement by saying, *Let's examine this in more detail. We know that _____ is the challenge. What strategies are you thinking about trying to strengthen this part of the lesson? What effect might these strategies have on the students' engagement in the lesson? What support might you need to implement these strategies?* LISTEN, paraphrase, and probe to understand the teacher's comments.	What strategies the teacher wants to try . . .

Step	Conversation Details	Conversation Notes
9	**Identify Other Areas for Improvement** Now it's the principal's turn to share other opportunities for growth. State what you observed, specifically during the lesson. For example, *During the lesson, I noted that 11 students did not respond to any questions posed to the class. They did not raise their hands, nor were they called upon to respond.* *Did you happen to notice this? What are your thoughts about it?* LISTEN *We know that one of the best ways to engage students in their learning is to involve them in responding to questions that push their thinking, and this was something you wanted to explore during the conversation today. What are some ideas you have for engaging all students in questioning and holding all students accountable for higher-order thinking in response to your questions?* LISTEN, paraphrase, and question to lead the teacher to reflect deeply about this portion of the lesson. Then ask, *Can I share with you what I have seen other teachers do to strengthen this aspect of their lessons?* *What are your thoughts about trying some of these ideas in your lessons?*	Write teacher responses here.

Part III: Collaborate on Next Steps and Close

Step	Conversation Details	Conversation Notes
10	**Collaboratively Determine Next Steps** Review the ideas shared by the teacher regarding the challenges she identified. Review the ideas generated to address the areas you observed and develop a plan to go forward to address both areas. For example, *Well, we have determined that you found _____ to be a challenge during the lesson, and you suggested _____ as a potential strategy to address it. We also discussed _____ as an area for growth from my observation, and you liked _____ strategy that other teachers have tried with success. Is that right?*	Action steps to be taken . . .

(Continued)

(Continued)

Step	Conversation Details	Conversation Notes
	What are your thoughts on going forward with these strategies? What support will you need from me and/or other staff members? When would be a good time to come in and see how it is going?	
11	**Close the Feedback Conversation** To close the conversation, ask the teacher if the feedback conversation was helpful and if it met her aim that she stated at the beginning. Also share how well the conversation met your aim for the conversation. Thank the teacher for her time and insight. End with a statement about the continued growth of the teacher and the process of instructional improvement at the school.	

Although reading through this protocol may have you thinking this process is time consuming, it is actually time efficient. We suggest that this protocol be shared with teachers at the beginning of the year and be used consistently for both formal and informal observational conversations. Having knowledge of the process for post-observation conversations lowers teacher anxiety about conversations with school leaders, and just as importantly, provides them think time to prepare for the conversation. Teachers then come to the conversation knowing the process, thus allowing them to fully engage in the conversation, and hear and contribute to the next steps going forward. With that, respond to the question below.

Which steps in the protocol resonated most with you? Make note of those parts, or the protocol in its entirety, as you plan to coach for instructional improvement. Furthermore, as you begin reading the next section on trust, be mindful that the protocol can only produce meaningful dialogue when trust has been built.

TRUST AND INSTRUCTIONAL LEADERSHIP

Leaders who successfully build and sustain organizational trust reap important benefits. Teachers in schools with high trust conduct their work from commitment to improving the learning lives of students, rather than from compliance with orders and directives. They collaborate with colleagues, and they feel a commitment to each other and the collective effort they have underway. Strong teacher morale is linked to collegial trust, necessary to create a high-performing organization.

Leaders who fail to cultivate a culture of trust between teachers and leaders and between and among teachers pay a heavy price. Without trust, teachers are unlikely to take risks, which robs them of discovering new ways of working with each other and with students. When trust is absent, people spend a lot of time in self-protection mode. Organizational energy is diverted from providing quality lessons to students to issues among the adults. Collegial sharing and collaboration in service of students suffers as teachers start to hold back and do just enough to get by. Not much of value can be accomplished if people are feeling this way, and when distrust takes hold, it grows and spreads, and it is difficult to repair (Tschannen-Moran, 2004).

Bryk and Schneider (2002), in their seminal work in Chicago schools, named four criteria for discernment of relational trust:

> **Leaders who successfully build and sustain organizational trust reap important benefits.**

➡ **Respect** comes in the form of basic civility and a willingness to listen deeply to what each person has to say. Parents, students, and teachers need opportunities to talk with and influence each other and to believe that they can positively affect educational outcomes.

➡ **Competence** is the sense that each party has the ability to carry out its appropriate roles and produce desired outcomes. This applies to both academic results and teacher–student relationships. When incompetence goes unchecked, it erodes trust and undermines shared efforts toward improving learning.

➡ **Personal regard** for others deepens relational trust. We are a social species, wired for relationships and reciprocity. Mutual support and caring fuel these associations. Extending ourselves to and for others is like making a deposit in the trust account, and the interest in this account compounds with each deposit.

➡ **Integrity** is the congruence between saying and doing. In trusting relationships, this means we believe that a sense of morality and ethics is operating in others and in the ways we are relating. Following through with agreements and commitments is a key aspect of integrity.

 Working on the Work

TEXT RENDERING PROTOCOL

Re-read the section on trust and instructional leadership. Choose a most significant sentence, phrase, and word, and record them in the chart or highlight them in your book. Examine your choices, make inferences, and apply them to the reflection question below the chart.

Trust and Instructional Leadership
Significant Sentence
Significant Phrase
Significant Word

What do your choices above tell you about your thinking regarding trust?

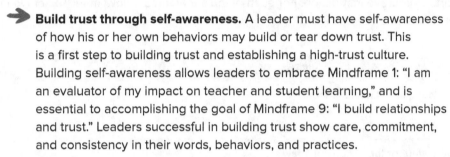

LEADERS BUILD TRUST

There are four ways you can build trust in your school community.

➤ **Build trust through self-awareness.** A leader must have self-awareness of how his or her own behaviors may build or tear down trust. This is a first step to building trust and establishing a high-trust culture. Building self-awareness allows leaders to embrace Mindframe 1: "I am an evaluator of my impact on teacher and student learning," and is essential to accomplishing the goal of Mindframe 9: "I build relationships and trust." Leaders successful in building trust show care, commitment, and consistency in their words, behaviors, and practices.

➤ **Build trust through thoughtful decision making.** Leaders are almost always on stage, being watched by teachers, students, administrators, and parents. Because words and actions set the tone for the rest of the school, leaders must practice staying composed and calm under pressure. Effective leaders do not succumb to pressure for a quick decision before they have the facts from all parties, and they understand that the best option is simply to say that you will look into the situation and follow up, as opposed to having to reverse and explain decisions that were made rashly.

➤ **Build trust by facing and addressing concerns.** Strong leaders have the courage to address concerns build trust. People expect strength and clarity from their leaders in this area. Correcting concerns and issues of staff competence involves talking to people individually, in person and in private, about the behavior or issue. This means setting, reviewing, and supporting people in meeting clear expectations. When working with a faculty member, ask questions, listen, and observe, and then provide honest and specific feedback that includes written documentation. Working with someone to discuss what he or she is not doing well is difficult; persistence and commitment are required for this time-consuming process. This approach ensures that teachers can trust in a respectful process. Your level of courage and skill in dealing with performance issues directly can have a direct impact on building and maintaining trust in your organization.

➤ **Build trust by recognizing the efforts of others.** Sincere and frequent expressions of appreciation help build trust. Turning your thoughts of gratitude into deliberate and frequent exchanges can help you build trust. Take a walk through your building and notice the displays of student work, teachers working with students, or staff assisting visitors. Take pictures to document the great work within your school. These observations can give you many ideas for individuals to thank. You can thank people in a variety of ways, through written notes, e-mails, and verbal exchanges. Handwritten notes can be especially powerful, and you are likely to see them hanging in classrooms or on desks afterward!

 A Work in Progress

TRUST-BUSTING

Consider the following potential trust-busters and commit to avoiding them. These actions can erode trust and derail your efforts to improve instruction. For each of the statements below, mark *Yes* or *No* in response to the question: *Have you ever . . . ?*

Have you ever . . .	Yes	No
1. Pretended to care, to listen, or to know something?		
2. Reprimanded the entire staff for the actions of a few?		
3. Given corrective feedback to a teacher in passing to save yourself time?		
4. Showed favoritism to certain individuals or groups?		
5. Failed to follow through on promises made?		
6. Flipped back and forth on decisions?		
7. Gossiped about staff members to other staff members?		
8. Disrespected students and their families with staff members?		
9. Shared confidential information?		
10. Exaggerated facts with staff members?		

REFLECTION

If you checked *Yes* to any of these trust-busting behaviors, you are human! But be mindful that a continued pattern of these behaviors can have a negative impact on the organizational trust in your school. Making a deliberate effort to avoid these trust-busters will improve staff trust in you and provide them a strong model for how they should conduct themselves as members of the school community.

ALL IN A DAY'S WORK

Consider the questions that follow and complete the chart to capture your thinking about strong instructional leadership.

Which of your current practices reflect strong instructional leadership?

➡ Place these practices in the KEEP section of the chart.

Which of your current practices are not aligned with strong instructional leadership?

➡ Place these practices in the STOP section of the chart.

What practices are you considering adding to your leadership to strengthen your instructional leadership?

➡ Place these practices in the START section of the chart.

ACTIONS	PRACTICES BASED ON MY LEARNING IN THIS MODULE:
KEEP	I will continue to . . .
STOP	I will stop . . .
START	I will start . . .

CONCLUSION

In this module, we focused on what current research is telling us about effective instructional leadership, specifically, that the impact of instructional leadership from the principal has a more pronounced impact on student learning than previously understood. With that in mind, we added that 80% of school leaders in a survey identified themselves as transformational leaders as opposed to instructional leaders. This is problematic due to the small effect size of transformational leadership and the much larger impact of instructional leadership. In this module, you were asked to consider the leadership practices you spend time on and whether these practices are the ones that have the greatest impact on student learning outcomes. Additionally, you read that your sense of self-efficacy, specifically for instructional leadership, may impact the decisions you make on where you spend your time. Strong instructional leaders are frequently in classrooms, observing instructional pedagogy, measuring impact on student learning, leading and organizing professional learning, and engaging in instructional coaching, feedback, and conversations frequently with teachers. Finally, trust was presented as a significant and essential component of instructional leadership, and we explored ways to build it for the sake of staff well-being and learning. Leaders who demonstrate care, commitment, and consistency build trust and impact the learning lives of students and staff positively.

Access resources, tools, and guides
for this module at the companion website:
resources.corwin.com/howleadershipworks

3

SUPPORT TEACHER CLARITY AND PROMOTE STUDENT ENGAGEMENT

LEARNING INTENTIONS

- I am learning about the four dimensions of teacher clarity: instruction, examples and explanations, guided practice, and assessment.

- I am learning about new research on student engagement that extends well beyond outward behaviors.

SUCCESS CRITERIA

- I can explain and recognize the relationship between teacher clarity and student engagement.

- I can use my instructional leadership skills to support and extend the work of teachers.

Most teachers would say that student engagement is the brass ring of teaching. After all, that's an item that appears on many classroom observation forms, often asking how many students were engaged during a teacher's lesson. The conventional wisdom is that those looking out the window are disengaged, while those sitting up straight and quietly taking notes are engaged. It is less common in an observation form to ask about teacher clarity. Do students understand what success looks like? Do they know what they are learning today and why it is relevant to them? We argue that student engagement and teacher clarity are intertwined, and clarity is the catalyst. Yet these two are rarely spoken of in the same conversation. It is as if there are two separate silos of teaching knowledge. Now, let us comingle them and magnify both.

Student engagement and teacher clarity are intertwined, and clarity is the catalyst.

A LEADER'S CHALLENGE

Amal is an elementary principal at a school located in a large city. The district Amal works in is one of the largest in the country. Because of its size, implementation of initiatives can be challenging. Her district is committed to two initiatives: fostering teacher clarity and promoting culturally responsive teaching. This principal lives by Mindframe 8: "I explicitly inform teachers and students what successful impact looks like from the outset." As she notes, "One of my major tasks as an instructional leader is to make sure that people have an idea of what success looks like."

In fact, her school is currently working on teacher clarity to strengthen their instructional practices. Amal has shared video examples of different elements of teacher clarity practices, inviting educators to engage in analyses in ways that are appreciative, as well as thought-provoking. In particular, she uses examples that highlight teacher clarity practices in culturally responsive teaching. At their meetings, she invites teachers to share their attempts and successes to promote collective learning. More recently, she and a team of teacher-leaders have adopted a check-in with students, asking them the following three questions:

➡ What are you learning today?

➡ Why are you learning it?

➡ How will you know you have learned it?

"We don't disaggregate the data, but we end up talking to about 10% of the student body each week," she said. Their weekly professional learning sessions begin with an update of the percentage of students who could answer each of the three questions.

"We look for trends and patterns over time," Amal explained. "What we're seeing is a steady rise in the numbers since the beginning of the year." However, Amal is wondering how to keep the momentum going. "As the year goes on, I don't want us to lose steam." Her leadership challenge is to convert early successes to ensure long-term change.

PAUSE AND PONDER

Which of Amal's leadership behaviors indicate that she is an effective instructional leader?

_____

_____

_____

_____

What advice do you have for Amal to capitalize on their early success?

TWO SIDES OF THE SAME COIN: CLARITY AND ENGAGEMENT

You can't have student engagement without teacher clarity. Think about it. We know that this century's breakthrough principle in education is that student ownership of learning is crucial to their success. The notion that simply stuffing knowledge into students' brains and hoping for the best has been thoroughly disproven (e.g., Chew & Cerbin, 2020). Learning is a more involved process than that, as students need to be able to acquire, consolidate, and store information (Almarode et al., 2021). A student's ability to move through these three phases of learning involves a complex brew of internal resources (attention, motivation) and external ones (instruction, assessment). To discuss a student's internal and external resources in isolation is to overlook the way these two constructs are inexorably woven together.

We know that student ownership of learning is crucial to their success.

 A Work in Progress

LEARNING SURVEY

How do you see yourself as a learner? Take the following survey about what you think about learning. Use the scales to mark what best represents your response to each statement.

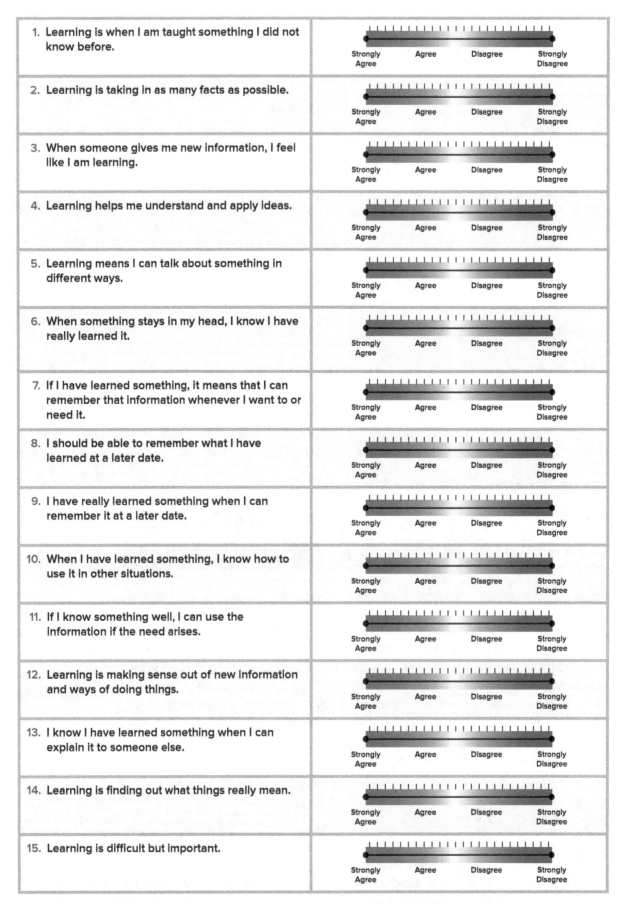

1.	Learning is when I am taught something I did not know before.
2.	Learning is taking in as many facts as possible.
3.	When someone gives me new information, I feel like I am learning.
4.	Learning helps me understand and apply ideas.
5.	Learning means I can talk about something in different ways.
6.	When something stays in my head, I know I have really learned it.
7.	If I have learned something, it means that I can remember that information whenever I want to or need it.
8.	I should be able to remember what I have learned at a later date.
9.	I have really learned something when I can remember it at a later date.
10.	When I have learned something, I know how to use it in other situations.
11.	If I know something well, I can use the information if the need arises.
12.	Learning is making sense out of new information and ways of doing things.
13.	I know I have learned something when I can explain it to someone else.
14.	Learning is finding out what things really mean.
15.	Learning is difficult but important.

Each statement has a scale: Strongly Agree — Agree — Disagree — Strongly Disagree.

Source: Fisher et al. (2019).

ONE SIDE OF THE COIN: TEACHER CLARITY

A challenge for instructional leaders is where to channel energy. *What works? With whom? Is it the right fit for my school?* While there are many possible initiatives that can be worthy candidates, we have found that teacher clarity ticks off all the boxes.

- **What works?** With an overall effect size of 0.84, an emphasis on teacher clarity is well worth the investment.

- **With whom?** Regardless of the grade level, discipline, or setting, teacher clarity is readily applicable and accessible to teachers. Whether a person is teaching Physical Education, running an individualized reading intervention program, or supporting students with intellectual disabilities in general education, teacher clarity is relevant to their practice.

- **Is it the right fit for my school?** Because the measurement of teacher clarity ultimately depends on student input, the discussions that result from monitoring this initiative inevitably give rise to other questions about curriculum, instruction, assessment, equity, teacher expectations, and opportunities to learn. In a nutshell, the work on teacher clarity becomes the gateway to surfacing other underlying issues and unstated assumptions.

Teacher clarity is an umbrella term that describes four crucial dimensions of teaching effectiveness. Interestingly, these four elements are tied to one another and should not be seen as separate and independent:

- **Organization of instruction** such that knowledge is built systematically and with intention (effect size = 0.64)

- **Explaining content** in ways that are accurate and developmentally appropriate (effect size = 0.70)

- **Providing examples and guided practice** that illuminate application, highlight errors to avoid, and allow students to talk on the learning using scaffolds as needed (effect size = 0.46)

- **Assessment of student learning** such that teachers make informed decisions about what's next, and students understand their own progress (effect size = 0.64)

We use learning intentions and success criteria to align these dimensions of teaching. Such coordination of effort is essential, especially when it comes to assessment. How often have we confronted a summative evaluation of our learning, only to discover that the content of the test didn't reflect our learning experiences?

Learning intentions and success criteria also have a student-facing benefit, as they provide learners with the cognitive toehold they need to master the content. In other words, they serve a priming effect that alerts the learner about what is to come. The learning intentions describe what it is that we want our students to learn. These are articulated in each lesson and change daily as the unit proceeds. With an effect size of 0.54, learning intentions can activate prior knowledge and prompt reflection.

➡️ *We are learning to apply the writer's use of figurative language and explain the impact on the reader.*

➡️ *We are learning where we live in the universe by planet, continent, and country.*

➡️ *We are learning to talk about pictures to share our ideas.*

Success criteria define what mastery looks or sounds like. It isn't getting a 90% or above on the end-of-unit exam, but rather are the ways students will know they have learned the skills or concepts.

➡️ *I can explain the parameters for a testable question in chemistry.*

➡️ *I can show my understanding of tempera techniques by completing a triptych painting using those techniques.*

➡️ *I can describe the skin's involvement in increasing and decreasing body temperature.*

Simply writing some learning intentions and success criteria on the board is not sufficient.

With an effect size of 0.88, success criteria hold a strong potential to accelerate learning. Techniques for success criteria include using I-can/we-can statements, such as those shown above. But other solid techniques include using rubrics, especially single-point rubrics that foster self-assessment, discussing exemplars, and modeling and thinking aloud about success criteria. As students and their teachers become more adept at these conversations, a natural outgrowth is that they collaborate to co-construct success criteria. The act of co-construction further cements the relationship between student ownership of their learning and their progress toward it.

 **A Work in Progress**

LEARNING INTENTIONS AND SUCCESS CRITERIA CHECK-IN

Revisit the learning intentions and success criteria listed at the beginning of this module. Self-assess your interim progress. What have you successfully learned so far? What do you still anticipate learning? What questions do you have so far?

What I Have Learned	What I Anticipate Learning	Questions I Still Have

LOOK-FORS AND LISTEN-FORS IN TEACHER CLARITY

It's helpful to know what to look for and listen for as you support teachers' efforts. Simply writing some learning intentions and success criteria on the board is not sufficient. Teachers also must talk about them, parse them with students, and find out what it is students know and don't know about the skills or concepts mentioned. Typically, these discussions last 2–3 minutes. Great discussion starters at the beginning of the lesson include:

➡ How much do you know about today's topic?

➡ Why is this topic important?

➡ What strategies will you need to use today to be successful?

➡ What do you expect to be easy about today's lesson? What will be hard?

Teachers should refer to the learning intentions and success criteria throughout the lesson. Many teachers do this before they shift to another instructional arrangement. A teacher who says, "Before we move back to the tables to work with your classmates, let's look again at what the purpose is," is doing just that.

Some use a mid-lesson technique called the muddiest point (Angelo & Cross, 1993). Pause the instruction and ask students, "What's been the muddiest point so far for you? What has been confusing or unclear?" This provides the teacher with feedback, but it also spurs students to reflect on their learning.

These same learning intentions and success criteria come back again near the end of the lesson to check in with students. It might be an exit ticket that again invites students to reflect on the lesson itself and their own learning:

➡ What do you need to know next? What wonderings do you have that I haven't addressed?

➡ What new knowledge did you acquire today?

➡ What strategy worked best for you today, and why?

Invite teachers to do similar reflections in the form of self-assessment. The Teacher Self-Reflection and Planning Guide provides a way for teachers to engage in the same kind of metacognitive thinking we know is so important for our students.

Include learning intentions and success criteria in your meeting agendas and in professional learning.

TEACHER SELF-REFLECTION AND PLANNING GUIDE

Learning Intentions

Teacher Practices Learning Intentions	Beginning B	Progressing P	Consistent C	Next Steps
1. Learning intentions are visible and usable for students.				
2. Learning intentions are discussed at the beginning, middle, and end of the lesson.				
3. Students are given time to reflect on and discuss the learning intentions.				
4. Connections are made to the learning intentions while students are engaged in the learning.				
5. Students are asked to monitor their progress using the learning intentions.				
6. Learning intentions are directly connected to the standard(s).				

Success Criteria

Teacher Practices Success Criteria	Beginning B	Progressing P	Consistent C	Next Steps
1. Success criteria are visible and usable for students.				
2. Success criteria are shared and clarified with students before, during, and after learning.				
3. Success criteria communicate *I will know I have learned it when I can . . .* with specific parts or steps needed for success.				
4. Success criteria include worked examples, exemplars, or models for clarity.				
5. Students are asked to use the success criteria to self-assess learning progress.				
6. Students are asked to provide feedback to peers using success criteria.				
7. Teacher uses success criteria to provide feedback to students.				

As an instructional leader, you want to know what to look for and what to listen for. In doing so, you enact Mindframe 8: "I explicitly inform teachers and students what successful impact looks like from the outset." Your ability to articulate your expectations in material ways assists teachers in understanding what success looks like. But let's not forget another vital mindframe in your leadership: "I build relationships and trust to make it safe to make mistakes and learn from others" (Mindframe 9). Make sure that you are leading by example. Include learning intentions and success criteria in your meeting agendas and in professional learning. Demonstrate to others that you are learning shoulder-to-shoulder with them. Solicit the same kind of feedback you'd like to see in classrooms. Instead of asking them about what they liked and didn't like (which often garners comments about the temperature of the room or the quality of the snacks), ask them about their learning. In the process, you'll also deepen your own understanding of the nuances of teacher clarity.

HOW DO YOU KNOW?

We started this module by noting that the alignment of instruction to assessment is essential to teaching with clarity. That's also the case when monitoring this initiative. Because here's the rub when it comes to teacher clarity: We don't get to decide if we are teaching with clarity. Our learners (young humans and older ones) let us know if we're successful. When you're in a classroom, stop asking students what they're *doing*. Your question turns their attention to the task: They're answering the questions at the end of a chapter, or they're completing the math exercises on page 104. Instead, ask them what they're *learning*. Then listen. Encourage them to put it into their own words, not just reading it verbatim off the whiteboard. Even better, ask them the three questions Amal shared at the beginning of the module:

When you're in a classroom, stop asking students what they're *doing*. Instead, ask them what they're *learning*.

➡ What are you learning today?

➡ Why are you learning it?

➡ How will you know you have learned it?

Further, consider monitoring student responses weekly. At Health Sciences High, we've done exactly that for several years now. The most unexpected occurrence, however, happened when the pandemic first began, and we had to pivot to distance learning. Within a few weeks' time, teachers began sharing Flipgrid videos of their students responding to these same three questions. In doing so, they struck on a new form of assessment to gauge student understanding, while also monitoring their own clarity. What had initially been a habit—weekly reporting and discussion—became a disposition. It was further evidence that we had moved from implementation to institutionalization of practices.

As teachers develop their skills pertaining to establishing clarity, it is useful to have means for providing actionable feedback. A feedback form like Quality Indicators for Learning Intentions and Success Criteria can equip teaching teams with a way to provide feedback to one another.

QUALITY INDICATORS FOR LEARNING INTENTIONS AND SUCCESS CRITERIA

Learning Intentions	Comments/Notes
States *I am learning . . .*	
Visible, usable, and age-appropriate for students	
Clear and concise	
Aligned to the standards: content, skills, and rigor	
Focuses on learning outcomes, not activities or assignments	
Does not contain success criteria	

Success Criteria	Comments/Notes
States *I know I have successfully learned when I can . . .*	
Visible, usable, and age-appropriate for students	
Contains the steps or process to successfully meet the learning intention	
Ordered with simple steps or parts first, then progresses to more complex steps or parts	
Clear and concise criteria	
If met, will truly result in success on the learning intention	
Focuses on doing or showing what I know	
Does not repeat the learning intention	
Serves as a checklist for students to self-assess where they are in the learning	
Can easily be used by students to give feedback to peers	

A Work in Progress

BEING INTENTIONAL

How intentional are you? Consider the actions you are considering in the beginning or continuing a teacher clarity initiative. For each of the statements below, indicate the extent to which it is part of your practice:

	Rarely	Sometimes	Always
I am mindful of how my actions and behavior impact how the staff are thinking and acting.			
I determine the impact I wish to have with staff and students before I act.			
I intentionally model the behaviors and actions I hope to see in staff.			
I seek evidence to inform my thinking and leading.			

THE OTHER SIDE OF THE COIN: STUDENT ENGAGEMENT

Ask an educator what student engagement looks like and sounds like, and they'll generally talk about outward behaviors: facing forward, still body, quiet mouths. Some will mention more academic signs, such as taking notes and answering questions. A few might add some of the deeper indicators, such as asking questions. For the most part, however, student engagement is largely defined in behavioral terms. As others have noted, we need to understand that there is *engagement in schooling* (compliance-oriented classroom behaviors) and *engagement in learning* (the cognitive and meta-cognitive strategies that propel learning) (Janosz, 2012). You can't talk about student engagement without contrasting it with disengagement.

ACTIVE ◄———————————————— PASSIVE ————————————————► ACTIVE

Disrupting	Avoiding	Withdrawing	Participating	Investing	Driving
Distracting others Disrupting the learning	Looking for ways to avoid work Off-task behavior	Being distracted Physically separating from group	Doing work Paying attention Responding to questions	Asking questions Valuing the learning	Setting goals Seeking feedback Self-assessment

DISENGAGEMENT	ENGAGEMENT

Source: Fisher et al. (2021a).

Let's look first at disengagement, which tends to be a bit more behavioral. Berry (2020) categorizes these in the following terms, from more passive to more active disengagement:

- **Withdrawing.** Students are not participating and may be uninterested and inactive but are not seeking to draw attention to themselves.
- **Avoiding.** A bit more active, students are off task and perhaps roaming around the room or fidgeting with materials.
- **Disrupting.** They are actively distracting or provoking another student, or actively challenging the teacher's authority.

These are pretty easy to spot and can definitely draw the ire of the teacher. There's lots of classroom management that is going to be necessary, and some disengagement behaviors may land in your office. We'll pause on disengagement for the moment and return to that in the next module section. Let's look at the other side of the continuum: engagement, noting again the range from more passive to active engagement.

- **Participating.** Students are completing tasks and following directions.
- **Investing.** Students are a bit more active, as they are asking content-related questions (not just seeking clarification on directions) and using their own interests and knowledge to understand.
- **Driving.** Students are actively seeking feedback so they can determine where conceptually they need to go next. They are monitoring their progress against goals and self-assessing to make decisions about their learning.

Now let's look at the middle of the continuum: passive disengagement and passive engagement. There isn't a whole lot that separates the two. Passively disengaged students are, for the most part, overlooked. Most teachers can tell you how some of their students have mastered the ability to hide in plain sight. More importantly, the measures of participation set a low bar that values compliance over learning. Now consider this question: Is your purpose instructional leadership or compliance leadership? Can't we do better?

 Working on the Work

FIVE-WORD SUMMARY

Scan the previous section, "The Other Side of the Coin: Student Engagement," and identify five words/phrases that resonate with you. List them below:

1. _____

2. _____

3. _____

4. _____

5. _____

Reflect on your list to consider themes related to your selection. Write two to three sentences that incorporate all your selected words/phrases.

_____

_____

_____

You might consider this to be your "elevator speech" about student engagement. Who would you like to share the elevator with?

_____

_____

_____

BUT WHY DO THEY DISENGAGE?

A maxim in the behavioral sciences is that all behavior (positive as well as problematic) has communicative intent. In other words, they seek to obtain or avoid something, and they happen for a reason. It's important to find out _why_ a student is disengaging. While they may fall somewhere on the disengagement continuum between passive and active, students disengage for some compelling reasons. And here's the big news: Four disengaged students in a classroom may have four very different reasons. A shortcoming of relying solely on classroom management techniques is that it assumes a narrow range of reasons.

Four disengaged students in a classroom may have four very different reasons.

Chew and Cerbin (2020) conducted a systematic review of the research literature on what they referred to as the cognitive barriers to teaching. They identified nine possible reasons why a student might disengage and recommendations for how to respond. We've summarized their findings in the following table, adding some teaching approaches and links with teacher clarity.

 A Work in Progress

RESPONSES TO COGNITIVE CHALLENGES

Each of the barriers cycles back in one way or another to teacher clarity. Mental mindset? Come back to the learning relevance. Metacognition and self-regulation? Some reflection might be in order. We've started a list of links to teacher clarity for you on the next page. How might you advise a teacher to utilize dimensions of teacher clarity to respond to a student who is disengaged?

Challenge	Barrier	Teaching Approach	Link to Teacher Clarity
1. Student mental mindset	Doesn't see purpose in the topic Doesn't believe they have the ability to learn it	Explain the value and importance of the learning, increase students' ownership of their learning, and explore the habits of minds and mindsets	Revisit relevance in the form of the question, "Why is that topic important to you?"
2. Metacognition and self-regulation	May be overconfident about their knowledge or skills and therefore doesn't devote attention to it	Create reflection assignments, teach students about planning, monitoring, and adjusting their learning, and use practice tests	Ask the student what they already know and pose a question that will be answered later in the lesson
3. Student fear and mistrust	The affective filter has been raised due to trauma, bullying, or a relationship with the teacher or peers has been damaged	Focus on teacher credibility, restructure feedback, and create a safe climate for learning and making mistakes	Assess the organization of the lesson and identify predictable routines that increase comfort; examples are trauma-sensitive and do not retraumatize the student
4. Insufficient prior knowledge	Prerequisite skills or concepts needed for mastery of new content are missing	Use initial assessments, provide lesson background knowledge and key vocabulary in advance, and use interactive videos	
5. Misconceptions	Possesses misconceptions about topic that remain even when exposed to accurate information	Use advance organizers, recognize common misconceptions for students at a specific age or in a specific content area, and invite students to justify their responses to that thinking	
6. Ineffective learning strategies	Utilizes suboptimal learning or study skills	Teach study skills, model effective strategies with think-alouds, and teach about spaced practice	
7. Transfer of learning	Can't apply knowledge to new or novel situations	Plan appropriate tasks, model application in different contexts, tailor feedback to include task processing	
8. Constraints of selective attention	Believes they can multitask or focuses on irrelevant stimuli	Increase teacher clarity, use breaks and re-orientation strategies, and teach students to avoid multitasking, especially with media	
9. Constraints of mental effort and working memory	Task is too complex or they are trying to memorize too much information	Organize information and chunk it, use both visual and auditory cues (dual coding), and use retrieval practice	

Source: Adapted from Frey et al. (2021).

ALL IN A DAY'S WORK

Consider the questions that follow and complete the chart to capture your thinking about how to lead your professional learning community effectively.

Which of your current practices align most strongly with the development of teacher clarity and student engagement practices?

➡️   Place these practices in the KEEP section of the chart.

Which of your current practices are not aligned with the development of teacher clarity and student engagement practices?

➡️   Place these practices in the STOP section of the chart.

What practices are you considering adding to strengthen your leadership aligned with the development of teacher clarity and student engagement practices?

➡️   Place these practices in the START section of the chart.

ACTIONS	PRACTICES BASED ON MY LEARNING IN THIS MODULE:
KEEP	I will continue to . . .
STOP	I will stop . . .
START	I will start . . .

CONCLUSION

Two worthy places to dedicate your instructional leadership are the related practices regarding teacher clarity and student engagement. The promise of each is in amplifying and magnifying the effect of the other. But rather than being caught up in the one-initiative-a-year trap, we advise using these together. Further, don't expect that these are one-and-done initiatives. The evolving nature of schools means that staff's experiences are not static. Center these as ongoing values and expectations and anticipate that these require continual nurturing to move them from habits to dispositions and from implementation to institutional norms.

Access resources, tools, and guides
for this module at the companion website:
resources.corwin.com/howleadershipworks

4

INVESTIGATE THE IMPACT OF TEACHING

LEARNING INTENTIONS

- I am learning how to help teachers determine their impact.

- I am learning how to determine my own impact.

SUCCESS CRITERIA

- I can support teachers in assessment development.

- I can guide conversations about impact using evidence.

- I can create tools to monitor my own impact.

The purpose of focusing on teaching is to ensure learning. In addition, part of our role is to help teachers monitor their impact while we monitor our own. For this reason, we will return to

Mindframe 1: I am an evaluator of my impact on teacher and student learning.

Mindframe 2: I see evidence and data as informing my impact and next steps.

Mindframe 3: I collaborate with peers, teachers, students, and families about my conceptions of progress and my impact.

Mindframe 10: I focus on learning and contribute to a shared language of learning.

To accomplish these mindframes, it's not enough to help teachers implement initiatives and ideas. We all need to know that they work. As we monitor, we have the responsibility to make adjustments and thus increase the impact of our efforts, both individually and collectively.

To determine whether we, as leaders and teachers, have had an impact, data are required. We must acquire or produce information that can be used to assess the outcomes of our efforts. These assessments need to align with the goals that we have for learning. Parenthetically, that's the goal of outcomes-based education (OBE), which has an effect size of 0.97. There is no specific style of teaching when it comes to

OBE. Instead, the focus is on clearly establishing the learning goals and then aligning resources to accomplish them.

As we engage in these recursive reviews of impact, we need to attend to the feelings and reactions of others. Recognize that data can be threatening for some educators and may have been used against people in the past. To create a climate that welcomes the impact conversation, there needs to be a lot of trust and willingness to confront things that are uncomfortable.

A LEADER'S CHALLENGE

There needs to be a lot of trust and willingness to confront things that are uncomfortable.

Carli is the director of an early childhood center. The center enrolls children as young as 3 months, and they can remain at the center until they enter kindergarten. Carli was visiting classrooms and noted that some students did not seem to notice and respond to the distress of others. She wondered if this was a pattern and if these learned behaviors were compromised because of interrupted learning experiences related to coronavirus disease or because of lack of attention to social and emotional learning within the program.

Volume 1 of the learning foundations document (California Department of Education, 2008), which lists the expectations for early childhood education, focuses on social and emotional development, language and literacy, English language development, and mathematics (other volumes focus on visual and performing arts, physical development, health, history, social sciences, and science). One expectation for social and emotional development is that "children respond sympathetically to a distressed person and are more competent at responding helpfully" (p. 9). Examples from the learning foundations document include the following:

- Asks a younger child, "Why are you crying?" and when told that she misses her mommy, communicates, "Don't worry—your mommy will come back soon."
- May communicate, "That's not fair!" in response to another child being excluded from the group.
- Helps a friend rebuild a fallen block tower.
- May come to the defense of a friend who is teased by a peer.
- Asks a teacher for bandages after a peer has fallen and scraped his knee.
- Asks, "Want some water?" of a friend who is coughing. (p. 9)

Carli met with the group of teachers and invited them to share their thinking on this expectation and the progress students had made over the course of the last year. Teachers shared random stories about children and their performance in this area. As one teacher noted, "I've never seen Josiah do this. But really, no one in my class does these kinds of things. I wonder if their families act this way."

Another teacher commented, "I see some of my students do this, but I'm thinking that I haven't really focused on this. I mean, I hope I model this, but I don't think that I've directly taught it. I've been really focused on concepts about print and letter recognition. Honestly, I'm not sure that we really have focused on the social and emotional skills of our students as much as we probably should."

The team decided that they needed to collect some baseline information. They conducted time samples, observing randomly selected children at 10-minute intervals. When there was an opportunity for a child to respond sympathetically, which did not occur at each interval, the adult noted the student's response. The team analyzed the samples and noted that there was a need to address this expectation.

Carli asked a team to develop a plan for implementation of social and emotional skills, identifying actions to implement and de-implement. Furthermore, she asked them to develop a monitoring system to determine their impact. A few months later, Carli met with teachers of these older students individually to explore their data and determine the impact they were having.

Each educator shared their baseline data, as well as their current data. Carli had conversations with her teachers about the impact they were having. Six of the teachers had a significant impact and were very pleased with their efforts.

As one of them said, "I just love these kids. They are so kind to each other. They are so . . . so sympathetic, and their responses are so sweet."

"You did that," Carli responded. "It's because of your efforts that they have learned to be sympathetic."

Two teachers did not have a strong impact on students' development of this learning expectation. In conversation with one of the teachers, Carli learned that the adult was cutting down the lessons because she was not sure how to fit it all in. Carli and the teacher had a good conversation about priorities and visited with other teachers who had revised their schedules to ensure that social and emotional development was prioritized.

As this teacher noted, "I don't want literacy and math to suffer. Are you sure that the students in all the classes are making progress?" Carli responded that there were good progress-monitoring data for all the classes and that the team should talk about this at their next meeting.

The other teacher, who did not have a strong impact on students' social and emotional development, noted that many of her students were missing the lessons because the specialists were scheduled simultaneously as the social-emotional learning.

"They are going to miss something," she said. "I don't really get to decide because the specialists tell us when they are going to be there. And you know I have a few students with really complex needs, and they're removed from the class several times a day."

Carli had not realized the impact of this. She said, "I'm so sorry. I should have known or noticed this. Can I have a couple of days to see if we can alter this and develop a better schedule? I need to talk with the specialist and their supervisor, and then I'd like to propose a few solutions, and you can decide if any of them are better than what is happening now."

PAUSE AND PONDER

How did Carli use data to engage her team members?

_____

_____

Which mindframes did you see present in Carli's efforts?

_____

_____

How can conversations about evidence improve the outcomes for students?

_____

_____

>>> Working on the Work

ANTICIPATION GUIDE

Are you ready to confront the data in front of you? For each of the statements that follow, mark true or false based on your current understanding. After reading about investigating impact, revisit your statements. Assess and consider the changes.

Before Reading		Change Statements	After Reading		Notes
True	False		True	False	
		1. Teachers can use the effect size tool to determine their impact.			
		2. The effect size allows teachers to determine a cause-and-effect relationship.			
		3. Building collective efficacy requires evidence of impact.			
		4. Success criteria help guide assessment efforts.			
		5. Informal walk-throughs are an effective and evidence-based way to determine impact.			

Note: Answers available on page 79.

HELPING TEACHERS DETERMINE THEIR IMPACT

In the introduction, we discussed effect sizes. An effect size is a quantitative measure of the strength of a phenomenon. In other words, it tells us how powerful something is in creating change. Furthermore, an effect size of 0.40 (calculated using Cohen's *d*) suggests that students gained a year's worth of growth for a year in school. It's the average impact of all the influences on learning. Now, remember that the effect sizes in published research typically have assessments that have been tested, and conditions for learning are often controlled. We use the 0.80 as a general guide with teachers using classroom assessments to assess and determine impact.

The effect size tool can be applied at the classroom level as well. Teachers can calculate effect sizes for their classes and individual students to determine the impact their instruction and intervention have had. This builds a teacher's sense of efficacy, which is a teacher's belief in their ability to positively impact student learning. Jerald (2007) noted that teachers with strong self-efficacy

→ Tend to exhibit greater levels of planning and organization

→ Are more open to new ideas and are more willing to experiment with new methods to better meet the needs of their students

→ Are more persistent and resilient when things do not go smoothly

→ Are less critical of students when they make errors

→ Are less inclined to refer a difficult student to special education (Protheroe, 2008, p. 43)

Over time, as teachers discuss the data and success with their peers, they develop collective teacher efficacy. Goddard et al. (2000) define collective teacher efficacy as "the perceptions of teachers in a school that the efforts of the faculty as a whole will have a positive effect on students" with teachers agreeing that "teachers in this school can get through to the most difficult students" (p. 480). Importantly, perceptions are formed based on our experiences. When teachers experience success collaborating with peers, and those collaborations improve teaching and learning, they notice. These accumulated data points become the collective efficacy researchers note is powerful (Hoy et al., 2002) and boasts an effect size of 1.36. We're just saying that the definition of success, on which these perceptions and thus collective teacher efficacy are built, should include student learning.

The process of calculating an effect size is fairly simple. However, before we discuss it, it's important to remember a few things:

1. **Lessons should have clear learning intentions.** It's hard to determine whether students have learned something if they (and their teachers) aren't sure what it was they were supposed to learn.

2. **Lessons should have clear success criteria.** The success criteria provide the tools necessary to assess learning. If the success criteria involve writing about

history, then learning must involve both writing and content area learning. Sometimes teachers conflate success criteria and are unable to determine if students have learned something, even when they have.

3. **The success criteria indicate what quality looks like.** To determine whether learning has occurred, students and teachers must know what success looks like. If students believe that good enough is sufficient, they may only reach for that level. When they understand what excellent work looks like, they can reach higher.

4. **Students should know where they stand in relation to the criteria for success.** When students have no idea whether they've done well, learning is compromised. Students should understand that learning is on a continuum, that errors are opportunities to learn, and that they can learn more.

With these four conditions in place, teachers are ready to examine the impact of the learning experience.

Pre-Assessment

It starts with a pre-assessment, or progress testing, as it is sometimes called. Without a pre-assessment, we cannot determine if learning occurred. When teachers only use post-assessments, such as end-of-unit tests, essays, or projects, they will know who has demonstrated the expected level of achievement (and who has not), but they won't know who learned because learning is a measure of change over time.

It's easy to overlook the pre-assessment and accept achievement as learning. But without strong pre-assessments, becoming a better teacher and designer of amazing learning situations is left to chance. For example, Gina Humphrey assessed her kindergarteners during the first week of November on their letter recognition, which is a worthwhile literacy skill. Students should recognize the letters of the alphabet, both lower and uppercase. Ms. Humphrey noted that all but four of her students could do so. That's their current achievement. It doesn't tell her anything about the impact of her teaching or the lessons she designed on their learning because she did not have a baseline.

What if most of the class had attended a transitional kindergarten class and already knew all of their letters? In that case, the time devoted to learning letters was a waste. What if none of her students knew their letters at the onset of the year? In that case, the lessons were probably powerful, and she might want to share them with her grade-level team. This kindergarten example highlights a missing part of many teachers' instructional practices. Failing to identify what students know and can do at the outset of a unit of study blocks any ability to determine if learning has occurred, and thus any ability for there to be a discussion about effective instruction and intervention.

Post-Assessment

Once the lessons have been completed, teachers administer the outcome measure. This opens the door to an investigation about impact. Did the lessons that were taught change students? That is learning.

When the pre- and post-test data are available, the effect size can be determined. A simple tool useful for this person can be found at https://bit.ly/leadershipVL.

As an example, Jayden Palmer had given students a pre-assessment as part of her algebra class. There were 14 items related to functions, the content that the class would be learning. As shown in Figure 4.1, several students scored perfectly on the pre-assessment and probably didn't need these lessons. Ms. Palmer wanted to build students' conceptual knowledge by having them engage in number talks and peer reviews of their work and planned to model using worked examples.

4.1 PRE- AND POST-ASSESSMENT DATA

Student	Time 1	Time 2	Effect Size
Munira	14	14	0.00
Mahammed	8	11	1.17
Nur-din	7	12	1.95
Emmanuel	7	13	2.34
Betsabe	9	14	1.95
Carlos	3	10	2.73
Nayeli	10	12	0.78
Aiyana	14	14	0.00
Deja	4	8	1.56
Rukaia	10	14	1.56
Heba	9	12	1.17
Axel	10	14	1.56
Georgina	12	14	0.78
Emir	10	14	1.56
Danielle	10	14	1.56
Matthew	9	12	1.17
Juan	10	14	1.56
Trinity	14	14	0.00
Dominic	6	11	1.95
Anthony	9	14	1.95
Nayelie	0	8	3.12
Andrea	11	11	0.00
Alex	7	13	2.34

Student	Time 1	Time 2	Effect Size
Perla	5	9	1.56
Saul	8	12	1.56
Kaci	9	12	1.17
Aye	12	14	0.78
Jonathan	9	9	0.00
Carla	9	12	1.17
Lizbeth	13	14	0.39
Ivan	8	10	0.78
Vivian	7	9	0.78
David	9	9	0.00
Alejandro	5	12	2.73
Fernando	8	12	1.56
Jazmin	3	9	2.34
Samuel	8	12	1.56
Angel	12	14	0.78
Jacob	14	12	−0.78
Ismael	7	10	1.17
Ezekiel	9	12	1.17
Liliana	4	10	2.34

	Time 1	Time 2	Effect Size
Average	8.62	11.90	1.28
STDEV	3.18	1.94	
AV Stdev		2.56	

In addition, Ms. Palmer gave students a post-assessment on the same standards and topics but with different items. Thus, the reason for some variation might be that students interpreted some items differently between the two assessments. The average pre-assessment score was 8.62. After two weeks of lessons on functions, the score for students in Ms. Palmer's class increased to an average of 11.90.

Is that an impact? It seems to be so, but was the effect noteworthy?

We need a little more information to know for sure. The standard deviation for the pre-assessment is 3.18, and the standard deviation for the post-assessment is 1.94. The average of the two is 2.56. When the effect size is calculated, it comes to 1.28, above our threshold of 0.80 for classroom assessment. Thus, Ms. Palmer can conclude her efforts to improve student knowledge about functions were successful. She can then infer that her actions—number talks, peer reviews, and worked examples—likely increased student learning. As a note of caution, effect sizes do not establish causation. Ms. Palmer cannot say with confidence that these specific actions caused the students to perform better, but she should be encouraged to share her approach with others so that they can determine the impact it might have on their students.

You may have noticed that the effect size is the average for the group. Ms. Palmer really should say that the efforts to improve understanding of functions worked on average. That's why we suggest that teachers calculate effect sizes for individual students.

In this case, most students are above the threshold of 0.80. Emmanuel, Carlos, Nayelie, Alex, Alejandro, Jazmin, and Liliana all had effect sizes over 2.0, suggesting that the lessons accelerated their understanding. For these students, Ms. Palmer should reflect on what was optimal about their learning.

Unfortunately, there was no effect on Andrea. As Ms. Palmer noted, "Andrea was out a lot, missing about 50% of the lessons. This is the last period of the day, and her mom picks her up a lot for medical appointments and therapy. I'm sure she needs it, but I think I should show her the achievement and see if we can work on a better schedule for her daughter."

Jacob experienced regression. His scores declined, and the effect size was −0.78. Ms. Palmer, reflecting on her instruction, said, "I thought he'd do better. I thought he was doing fine with the lessons. For some reason, this didn't work, and I owe it to him to schedule some additional instruction so that I can figure out what they need from me."

At the collective level, teachers can meet in grade-level groups or course-alike teams and engage in the same process. For example, the fourth-grade team at Country Ranch Elementary School was focused on improving students' public speaking. They collaborated on a series of lessons that included analyzing videos of effective and ineffective public speakers, focusing on prosody (e.g., intonation, pauses, emphasis), and preparing and practicing speeches. At one of their grade-level meetings, they compared assessment results. Each teacher had submitted pre-assessment scores and averages, and standard deviations had been calculated. Six weeks later, they collected benchmark data to make decisions about their impact.

 A Work in Progress

DATA VISUALIZER

In addition to the effect size table, the achievement and progress tool provides a data visualizer (see Figure 4.2). The lower left suggests minimal progress and low achievement. Students in this quadrant are of significant concern. The lower right suggests progress but not yet strong achievement. Teachers are having an impact and need to keep focused on the learning of these students. Students in the upper left quadrant achieved well but didn't make a lot of progress. Traditionally, they are neglected because they are already achieving. Students in the upper right quadrant have made a lot of progress and are achieving well. This is a cause for celebration.

4.2 **PROGRESS AND ACHIEVEMENT**

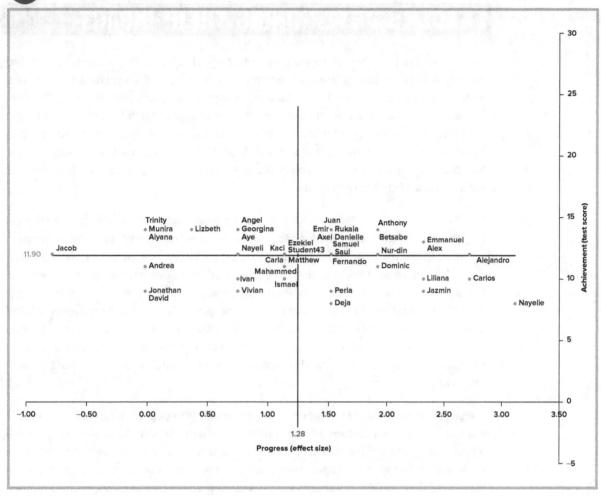

What actions would you suggest for each of the quadrants?

Low achievement but minimal progress:

_____

_____

Low achievement but good progress:

_____

_____

High achievement but minimal progress:

_____

_____

High achievement but good progress:

_____

_____

LEADERS DETERMINING THEIR IMPACT

School leaders have two roles constantly in play. The first is helping teachers determine their impact using student achievement indicators, capturing student voice, and making informal checks for understanding before, during, and after lessons. The second is being accountable for determining their own impact on the learning of staff and students. Furthermore, leader impact starts with the essential elements of strong implementation planning, which we discuss in Module 10. If done well, your implementation plan will provide the tools you need to measure your impact on the learning and achievement of staff and students.

As noted in the tool in Module 10, the plan includes "active ingredients," or steps in the strategy of retrieval practice. To determine the success of the implementation activities in the third column, a leader can create an evidence collection tool to determine the impact of their support over the short, medium, and long terms. Review the evidence collection tool that follows, developed using the list of "active ingredients" in the retrieval practice implementation plan (Module 10). This tool is offered here as a sample way of collecting implementation evidence on a preferred strategy you are trying. This is just one way to collect implementation evidence, but an effective practice to determine the leader's or implementation team's impact on staff learning.

We suggest using the tool at regular intervals during the year to determine progress in the number and percentage of staff meeting the expectations for the various "active ingredients" outlined for successful retrieval practice. After each evidence collection walk, the implementation team should analyze the data, reflect on the impact or lack thereof of their efforts to support staff in learning about this practice, and then make decisions about what support and learning are required to address any implementation gaps noted in the data.

EVIDENCE COLLECTION TOOL FOR RETRIEVAL PRACTICE (AN EXAMPLE)

Active Ingredient 1: Connects to previous learning	Not Attempted	Attempted	Proficient
Start the lesson with retrieval practice, to be called Smart Connect, which replaces the previous Connect starter activity.			
Focus on spaced retrieval of information from previous lessons.			
Takes no more than 5 minutes.			

Active Ingredient 2: Consolidate immediate learning	Not Attempted	Attempted	Proficient
Introduce retrieval practice at the end of each lesson to be called Smart Consolidate, which replaces previous Consolidate activity.			
Focus on the retrieval of information from the lesson that has just ended.			
Takes no more than 5 minutes.			

Active Ingredient 3: Retrieve from memory	Not Attempted	Attempted	Proficient
Smart Connect activity is from memory only—no books or notes.			
Smart Consolidate activity is from memory only—no books or notes.			

Active Ingredient 4: Quizzing	Not Attempted	Attempted	Proficient
Both Smart activities take the form of quiz questions on factual material, vocabulary, or application of key information.			
A range of formats are used to present the retrieval practice, that is, retrieval grids and presentation slide templates.			
Answers are provided, and students self-check.			

Active Ingredient 5: Consistent format	Not Attempted	Attempted	Proficient
Smart logo to be displayed on slides or materials to promote recognition and metacognition by students.			

 A Work in Progress

ANALYSIS OF IMPACT

Review the worked example that follows the initial evidence collection on the implementation of retrieval practice. Note the raw number and percentage of staff proficient in the active ingredient listed and then the number and percentage of staff attempting or not attempting that required ingredient. Answer the reflection questions that follow as if this were your school.

EVIDENCE COLLECTION TOOL FOR RETRIEVAL PRACTICE

Active Ingredient 1: Connect to previous learning	Not Attempted	Attempted	Proficient
Start the lesson with retrieval practice, to be called Smart Connect, which replaces the previous Connect starter activity.	6 (20%)	11 (37%)	13 (43%)
Focus on spaced retrieval of information from previous lessons.	12 (40%)	10 (33%)	8 (27%)
Takes no more than 5 minutes.	20 (67%)		10 (33%)

Active Ingredient 2: Consolidate immediate learning	Not Attempted	Attempted	Proficient
Introduce retrieval practice at the end of each lesson to be called Smart Consolidate, which replaces previous Consolidate activity.	20 (67%)	5 (16.5%)	5 (16.5%)
Focus on the retrieval of information from the lesson that has just ended.	20 (67%)	5 (16.5%)	5 (16.5%)
Takes no more than 5 minutes.	30 (33%)		0 (0%)

Active Ingredient 3: Retrieve from memory	Not Attempted	Attempted	Proficient
Smart Connect activity is from memory only—no books or notes.	15 (50%)	10 (33%)	5 (16.5%)
Smart Consolidate activity is from memory only—no books or notes.	13 (43%)	15 (50%)	2 (7%)

Active Ingredient 4: Quizzing	Not Attempted	Attempted	Proficient
Both Smart activities take the form of quiz questions on factual material, vocabulary, or application of key information.	12 (40%)	15 (50%)	3 (10%)
A range of formats are used to present the retrieval practice, that is, retrieval grids and presentation slide templates.	14 (47%)	10 (33%)	6 (20%)
Answers are provided, and students self-check.	14 (47%)	8 (26.5%)	8 (26.5%)

Active Ingredient 5: Consistent format	Not Attempted	Attempted	Proficient
Smart logo to be displayed on slides or materials to promote recognition and metacognition by students.	10 (33%)	7 (23%)	13 (43%)

In what areas do you note the highest percentages of proficiency? And the lowest?

What might be the reasons for these numbers?

If this were your school, what would you do next to support teachers in getting to deeper levels of implementation of retrieval practice?

What process would you use to share the data with them?

ALL IN A DAY'S WORK

Consider the questions that follow and complete the chart to capture your thinking about how to lead your professional learning community effectively:

Which of your current practices most strongly align with investigating the impact of teaching?

➡   Place these practices in the KEEP section of the chart.

Which of your current practices are not in alignment with investigating the impact of teaching?

➡   Place these practices in the STOP section of the chart.

What practices are you considering adding to strengthen your leadership aligned with investigating the impact of teaching?

➡   Place these practices in the START section of the chart.

ACTIONS	PRACTICES BASED ON MY LEARNING IN THIS MODULE:
KEEP	I will continue to . . .
STOP	I will stop . . .
START	I will start . . .

CONCLUSION

In this module, we explored teaching; however, we did not spend a lot of time on instructional strategies. Yes, teachers need strategies, and they need instructional plans, but the role of the leader is not to tell teachers which strategies work. There is no one right way to teach. Instead, leaders should help teachers determine if their instructional interventions made an impact. Furthermore, leaders should help groups of teachers determine whether they made an impact. In doing so, leaders can foster individual and collective efficacy. However, leaders do not limit their focus to others. They also determine their own impact and implement changes to increase the impact that they have on teaching and learning.

*Answer key to the anticipation guide: (1) True, (2) False, (3) True, (4) True, (5) False

Access resources, tools, and guides
for this module at the companion website:
resources.corwin.com/howleadershipworks

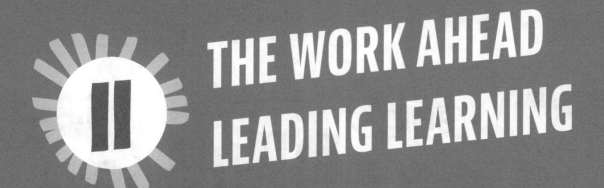

THE WORK AHEAD
LEADING LEARNING

Learning is affected by the climate and culture in both classrooms and schools. Schools with a healthy, supportive climate get better learning outcomes from students. The effect size for school climate is 0.44, thus showing a potential to positively impact learning. Every school has a climate and culture. Some of these are toxic and neglected, whereas others are nurtured and shaped. In fact, the behaviors and actions of individuals within the school or district create the climates on a daily basis. As Disney says, we must create the magic every day.

Importantly, climate is established by leaders and practiced and maintained daily by educators. As the poet Rumi, who died in 1273, noted: Fish begins to stink at the head, not the tail. This has become the leadership proverb, "The fish rots at the head." It may not be true as the guts probably stink first, but the saying has stuck as the world recognizes the value of leaders in creating the conditions for work and learning to occur.

Leaders provide these conditions in several formats, from the interactions we have with educators, to the messages we share, to the collaborative teams we support, to the feedback we provide. In fact, leaders are always "on." Our colleagues are always watching us, taking note of our actions and what we say. Returning to Disney's philosophy, we are always "on stage," and our actions matter.

In this part, we focus on

- Building a learning-focused school climate (Module 5)
- Empowering professional learning communities (Module 6)
- Ensuring growth-oriented feedback (Module 7)

5

BUILD A LEARNING-FOCUSED SCHOOL CLIMATE

LEARNING INTENTIONS

- I am learning about the emotional and academic climate of schools and classrooms.

- I am learning about the value of high expectations as a tool for opportunities to learn.

SUCCESS CRITERIA

- I can describe elements of school climate that promote learning for each student.

- I can use my leadership skills to support and extend the work of educators as they focus on school climate.

School climate can have a positive effect on student learning. With an effect size of 0.44, it has the potential to ensure learning. School climate refers to the social and environmental conditions that allow students to explore, reach aspirations, and learn about themselves and others. Although the terms *school culture* and *school climate* are sometimes used interchangeably, they are related but not synonymous. School culture is what you do; it is the way things work in a school, including rules, procedures, and so on. But school climate is how it *feels*. These perceptions are likely to differ between individuals.

> School culture is what you do; school climate is how it *feels*.

Consider the culture and climate of a busy and unfamiliar place that you don't have much experience with. The four of us travel a lot, so moving through the Transportation and Safety Administration (TSA) checkpoint at the airport is routine. Even though there are lots of rules and procedures, we're familiar with them and can correctly anticipate what will happen and in what order. However, there are always people around us who are infrequent travelers. For them, the TSA line can be intimidating. If you travel a lot, take a moment to reflect on the number of times you have seen a kind TSA agent assisting an inexperienced traveler. The rules and procedures are still in place, but the perception of that traveler was transformed because an agent saw the person's need and moved to action. We have seen this happen time and again, and it affects our perception, too. Helping has an echo effect that goes beyond the individual traveler. It reaffirms our own confidence that we are in the hands of conscientious public servants. A positive school climate similarly impacts those who need support, as well as those who witness the support. And isn't that what we seek to accomplish every day?

A LEADER'S CHALLENGE

Song is the principal of a middle school located in a region that had historically been rural. However, rapid development over the last decade has led to a sharp rise in enrollment as well as something of a cultural divide in the community. Long-time multigenerational residents mixed with new arrivals drawn to the region because of work opportunities are reshaping what schooling looks like. However, the changes are not always welcome. Song often hears a handful of veteran teachers referring to "the good old days" before the community's growth. Other educators hired during the enrollment boom are struggling to forward innovative methods. The strife internally and in the community is taking its toll on the student body, too. There's an undercurrent of divisiveness that has left the principal unsettled.

Song understands the importance of voice in decision making. Drawing on Mindframe 5, "I embrace challenge, and I support teachers and students in doing the same, not just doing our best," the principal met with several groups to gather multiple perspectives, including teachers, support staff, and community members. However, it was the meeting with a group of students that was most insightful. "These young people made it known that they had little input in decisions that directly affected them. They also felt that teachers and staff didn't really know them as individuals. I was surprised to hear that."

Song shared her takeaways from the student meeting at the next professional learning meeting. To gather some preliminary data to work with, she proposed they begin with a student survey designed to gather information on student voice and decision making (https://surveys.quagliainstitute.org). A few weeks later, the results of the survey, which were disaggregated by gender, grade level, and ethnicity, were shared with the staff. "This proved to be a turning point for us, regardless of our own experiences," she said. Here's what they learned:

- ➤ 94% of students said their families are their primary inspiration to do better in school.

- ➤ 63% of students felt accepted at school.

- ➤ 35% said that students respected one another.

- ➤ 32% said they had a voice in decision making at school.

"We had no idea that families were such an important support for the work we do," she explained. "And we were disheartened to see that issues of belonging, respect, and leadership were so low." Song's leadership challenge is to rebuild her school's climate.

PAUSE AND PONDER

What effective leadership actions did Song take?

_____

_____

_____

What advice do you have for her next steps?

_____

_____

_____

THE INTENTIONALLY INVITING SCHOOL LEADER

There's an adage that the teacher sets the climate for the class. The same is true for leaders at the school or district level. Your influence on the "weather" is profound and starts with fostering a sense of belonging among teachers. Affiliation is a strong motivator for doing more and doing better. The truth is that we try a bit harder on behalf of a group we feel an allegiance to.

Purkey and Novak (1996) described teachers in four categories across two constructs: intentionality and invitation:

- **Intentionally uninviting teachers** create a hostile learning environment. Their students are never sure where they stand (blessedly few, thank goodness).

- **Unintentionally uninviting teachers** hold themselves at an emotional distance from their students and hold low expectations of them.

- **Unintentionally inviting teachers** are eager and positive but don't have much insight into what works for them and what doesn't. This leaves them vulnerable to setbacks, and in time they may become uninviting teachers.

Intentionally inviting teachers have a strong sense of their practice and are insightful about the psychological and instructional moves they make to foster learning. That self-knowledge informs their confidence, and they are a steady presence to their students.

School leaders can find themselves on the continua of intentionality and invitation. Your interactions with teachers, both the strong ones and those who need more guidance and support, set the climate for your school. And much like observing a helpful public servant, there is a benefit among the adults, even those who are not direct beneficiaries. Your intentionality about inviting teachers to become members of the school community sets an important tone that has a ripple effect across students and families. If we want to develop caring educators, they need to know they are cared for and cared about.

 **A Work in Progress**

INTENTIONALITY OF LEADERSHIP

Intentionally Uninviting Leaders	Intentionally Inviting Leaders
• Are judgmental and belittling • Display little care or regard • Are uninterested in the lives or feelings of teachers • Isolate themselves from school life • Seek power over teachers	• Are consistent and steady with teachers • Notice learning and struggle • Respond regularly with feedback • Seek to build, maintain, and repair relationships
Unintentionally Uninviting Leaders	**Unintentionally Inviting Leaders**
• Distance themselves from teachers • Have low expectations for teachers • Don't feel effective and blame teachers for shortcomings • Fail to notice teachers learn or struggle • Offer little feedback to teachers	• Are eager but unreflective • Are energetic but rigid when facing problems • Are unaware of what works in their practice and why • Have fewer means for responding when teacher learning is resistant to their usual methods

Source: Adapted from Purkey & Novak (1996).

Review the chart on intentional leadership. Where do you reside most often? What do you seek to strengthen?

A SUPPORTIVE SCHOOL CLIMATE BEGINS WITH RELATIONSHIPS

A positive school climate is one where students feel physically and psychologically safe, where they feel that they belong, and where they are busy with the business of learning. An emotionally safe school environment is foundational; it is nearly impossible to learn in a place that feels threatening. Trust and belonging form the core of an emotionally safe environment. Effective schools foster a web of relationships among and between students and staff so that no one feels alone or unsupported. This web of relationships is called *social capital*. The term has its roots in economics and describes the ways members invest in one another. A student in a school community where there is high social capital sees allies and supporters inside and outside of school.

Social capital in schools is linked to the academic success of students.

Importantly, social capital in schools is linked to the academic success of students. Thus, one longitudinal study of 100 elementary schools found that the intangible quality of its network of relationships made a difference in academic outcomes in reading and math (Bryk et al., 2010). Another study of social capital in high schools determined that higher rates were associated with higher graduation rates and standard-based test scores (Salloum et al., 2017). Interestingly, the socioeconomic status of the school or the extent to which the school was well-resourced did not hold the same predictive power. Thus the authors defined four characteristics of social capital:

➡ **The normative behaviors of the school** (how problems are resolved and decisions are made)

➡ **Relational networks** (the triangle of interpersonal relationships between teachers, students, and their families)

➡ **Trust in parents** (the belief of school staff that parents and teachers work together effectively to achieve goals)

➡ **Trust in students** (the belief of school staff that students work together with teachers effectively to achieve goals)

To measure social capital, they used a survey tool you can easily deploy to determine what teachers, students, and parents perceive about the climate.

SOCIAL CAPITAL SCALE

Social Capital Scale Items	Strongly Disagree					Strongly Agree
Teachers in this school have frequent contact with parents.	1	2	3	4	5	6
Parental involvement supports learning here.	1	2	3	4	5	6
Community involvement facilitates learning here.	1	2	3	4	5	6

(Continued)

(Continued)

Social Capital Scale Items	Strongly Disagree					Strongly Agree
Parents in this school are reliable in their commitments.	1	2	3	4	5	6
Teachers in this school trust the parents.	1	2	3	4	5	6
Teachers in this school trust their students.	1	2	3	4	5	6
Students in this school can be counted on to do their work.	1	2	3	4	5	6
Students are caring toward one another.	1	2	3	4	5	6
Parents of students in this school encourage good schooling habits.	1	2	3	4	5	6
Students respect others who get good grades.	1	2	3	4	5	6
The learning environment here is orderly and serious.	1	2	3	4	5	6

Source: Goddard (2003).

 **A Work in Progress**

SOCIAL CAPITAL SCALE REFLECTION

Reflect on the 11 items in the social capital scale. Which items would you predict are current strengths at your school? What items do you predict will reveal a growth opportunity?

Predicted Strengths	Predicted Growth Opportunities

If you administer the scale later, look again at your predictions and compare them to your results.

Actual Strengths	Actual Growth Opportunities

THE SCHOOL CLIMATE PERMEATES CLASSROOMS

The climate of the school is directly affected by the climate of its classrooms. Much has been written about the importance of classroom climate in learning. These qualities allow children and young people to grow academically as they pursue their aspirations (Ruzek et al., 2016):

➡ **Relatedness** through demonstration of interest in a student's life

➡ **Providing reliable structures and boundaries** by creating fair and consistent expectations and rules that govern interactions

➡ **Autonomous conditions** that provide choice and opportunities to make decisions that matter

➡ **Optimism about the student,** which is infused in communication with the student about beliefs in them as learners and people

➡ **Emotional support,** especially in acknowledging feelings and assisting them in processing emotions

However, the available emotional support in a classroom is the *average* of that which is available to each student. Remember the warm feelings we described when watching a helpful TSA agent assist an inexperienced traveler? In such cases, we indirectly benefit from the emotional support provided even though we are not its recipients. Likewise, a teacher who witnesses your support of a colleague perceives a higher degree of emotional support available to them. It works the other way, too. When a student witnesses a classmate receiving little or no emotional support from an adult, the observer also perceives a decline in available support for themselves. It's kind of like secondhand smoke. Breathing in psychologically toxic fumes has an echo effect on all those in the environment.

Educators are humans before they are teachers. It's natural that we are going to like some students more readily than others. Without intending to, it's possible that some students receive less emotional support than others. And troublingly, there is a relationship between emotional support and student achievement. Good (1987) reviewed 20 years of research on classroom relationships to examine the differential ways high- and low-achieving students receive emotional support from their teachers. His findings appear below:

Low-Achieving Students	High-Achieving Students
• Are criticized more often for failure	• Are criticized less often for failure
• Are praised less frequently	• Are praised more frequently
• Receive less feedback	• Receive more feedback
• Are called on less often	• Are called on more often
• Have less eye contact with the teacher	• Have more eye contact with the teacher
• Have fewer friendly interactions with the teacher	• Have more friendly interactions with the teacher
• Experience acceptance of their ideas less often	• Experience acceptance of their ideas more often

If you're thinking to yourself, "Well, that was a long time ago. Surely things have changed?" the answer, sadly, is no. Good and colleagues updated their research review in 2018 and drew similar conclusions.

The relative amount of emotional support each student receives communicates the teacher's expectations. We'll discuss teacher expectations in more detail in the next section. But for now, it is important to note your role as a school leader. The goal is not to catch teachers in their failing moments, but rather to help them notice and then change their interactions with students receiving less support. One of the ways to embody Mindframe 2, "I see evidence and data as informing my impact and next steps," is to take action. When a teacher struggles with particular students, you hear about it. Often those students are frequent visitors to the office. Recognize this as data. Assist the teacher by taking data for them during arranged classroom visits about their interactions (see the tool below). It isn't always comfortable to look at this kind of evidence, but it is something that courageous leaders do because it fuels improvement. As the teacher implements changes and actively re-recruits the student(s), note the change in interactions and the student(s)' learning. Talk about this with the teacher as well. This is an extension of the ways that you are intentionally inviting as a school leader. Keep track of the following:

➡ **Patterns and trends in the data:** What am I seeing across time, across the grade level or department, or across the school?

➡ **Changes in identified students:** How have increased interactions impacted students and their learning? How has this changed the teacher experience?

➡ **Actions and next steps:** Based on the data, what do I still need to do?

NOTICING INTERACTION PATTERNS

Interaction	Student 1	Student 2	Student 3
Did the teacher greet the student by name when they entered the (virtual or in-person) classroom?			
How many times did the teacher use their name (not as a correction) during the session?			
Did the teacher ask them a critical thinking question related to the content?			
Did the teacher ask them a personal question?			
Does the student expect all or only some of the students to succeed?			
Does the teacher group by ability in the class and show that they have lower expectations of success for some of these groups?			

Interaction	Student 1	Student 2	Student 3
Does the teacher have many explanations for why they cannot succeed with some students?			
Did the teacher pay them a compliment?			
How many times did the teacher provide them with praise for learning performance?			

Source: Fisher et al. (2021b).

 ## Working on the Work

FOUR A'S PROTOCOL

Use the 4 A's text protocol developed by the National School Reform Initiative to critically analyze the section you just read above titled "The School Climate Permeates Classrooms."

1. What do you **Agree** with in the text?	
2. What **Assumptions** do the authors of the text hold?	
3. What do you want to **Argue** with in the text?	
4. What parts of the text do you want to **Aspire** to (or **Act** upon)?	

A LEARNING-FOCUSED SCHOOL CLIMATE

Warmth and unconditional positive regard don't guarantee learning; rather, they are catalysts for learning. The expectations for future performance we hold for students have a direct influence on learning, with an effect size of 0.42. What we choose to teach (and not teach) and to whom we teach it (and who we exclude) have a ripple effect across the academic career of a student. We tell students that working hard in school will yield opportunities for them, but do we deliver?

TNTP (formerly The New Teacher Project) examined representative elementary, middle, and high schools in several districts. Each school chosen represented either the top 50% or the lower 50% of student achievement within the district, by grade level (2018).

The researchers examined several data points over the course of a school year in core subject areas, as well as career and technical education. These data points included

- Assignment analyses of nearly 5,000 tasks
- 20,000 student work samples
- Nearly 1,000 classroom observations of instruction
- 30,000 surveys measuring engagement as reported by students (e.g., "I felt excited about learning")
- 30,000 surveys measuring their perceptions of the lesson's worth (e.g., "Class was about something important to my future")
- Interviews with teachers about their perceptions and expectations for student success against the standards (e.g., "my students need something different than what is outlined in the standards")

The researchers found that in schools that leveraged four key resources—high expectations, strong instruction, deep engagement, and grade-level assignments—students who started the year below grade level caught up with peers within 6 months. These schools were likely to fall in the top 50% of their district.

However, 38% of classrooms where the majority were students of color never received a grade-level appropriate assignment. These were more often in schools in the lower 50% of district achievement. Only 44% of teachers surveyed believed that their students could master the standards. In addition, the projected academic trajectory for these students was ominous: students who began the year substantially below grade level and had a 5-year string of low expectation classrooms were projected to be 40 months behind similarly achieving peers who had a 5-year sequence of high-expectation classrooms.

We do not believe that caring educators intentionally lower their expectations of their students. However, over time, expectations can drift and are reinforced by local practices (e.g., the teacher across the hall). Challenge teachers to examine the quality of upcoming assignments using the criteria developed by TNTP:

- **Content:** Does the assignment align with the expectations defined by grade-level standards?
- **Practice:** Does the assignment provide meaningful practice opportunities for this content area and grade level?
- **Relevance:** Does the assignment give students an authentic opportunity to connect academic standards to real-world issues and/or contexts?

As an additional resource, you'll find subject-specific assignment analysis rubrics at https://tntp.org/student-experience-toolkit/view/assignment-review-protocols to assist teaching teams in examining their own assignments.

ALL IN A DAY'S WORK

Consider the questions that follow and complete the chart to capture your thinking about how to effectively lead your professional learning community.

Which of your current practices most strongly align with fostering a learning-focused school climate?

➡ Place these practices in the KEEP section of the chart.

Which of your current practices are not in alignment with fostering a learning-focused school climate?

➡ Place these practices in the STOP section of the chart.

What practices are you considering adding to strengthen your leadership aligned to fostering a learning-focused school climate?

➡ Place these practices in the START section of the chart.

ACTIONS	PRACTICES BASED ON MY LEARNING IN THIS MODULE:
KEEP	I will continue to . . .
STOP	I will stop . . .
START	I will start . . .

CONCLUSION

School climate begins with the school leader's intentionality to become an inviting and supportive pacesetter. As a leader, you must be an evaluator of impact with the goal of achieving a better school climate, as stated in Mindframe 1. In doing so, you set the scene for teachers to extend their support to students and families. Intentionality also requires that emotional supports are sought, fostered, maintained, and repaired. Having said that, emotional support on its own will only get you so far. The true propellent is holding high expectations for students. However, holding high expectations without emotional support alienates students. You need both to accomplish the breakthrough results you are seeking.

Access resources, tools, and guides
for this module at the companion website:
resources.corwin.com/howleadershipworks

6

EMPOWER PROFESSIONAL LEARNING COMMUNITIES

LEARNING INTENTIONS

- I am learning about the characteristics of a high-performing PLC.

- I am learning about the powerful influence collective teacher efficacy has on student learning.

SUCCESS CRITERIA

- I can create the conditions needed to foster an effective PLC.

- I can use my leadership skills to support and extend the work of teams.

Professional learning communities (PLCs) form the heart of instructional improvement processes in a school. Effective school leaders leverage the power of this network to lead learning by fostering the collective wisdom of teachers to strengthen instruction and address structural and institutional barriers inhibiting the progress of some students.

That's the promise of a PLC. But mention PLCs during a school leaders' meeting, and you're likely to elicit moans and sighs. Too often, the reality is that the schoolwide PLC (and there really is only one) has devolved into grade-level or department meetings that remain isolated from one another. There's some conversation about test scores, subsequent discussion about the reasons why the results weren't as positive as it was hoped, and then a switch to talking about which books to order for an upcoming unit. Someone writes up a brief agenda and minutes and submits them, and they are never looked at again.

A LEADER'S CHALLENGE

Yesinia is an assistant principal in her first year at an elementary school whose test scores regularly earn high marks on parenting and real estate websites. However, the standards-based test scores belie an ugly truth: They mostly get by because many students have access to a wide array of outside, often private, supports. Many students in the school have private tutoring and music lessons, and they travel nationally and internationally. The students who don't have access to these same privileges flounder and are often regarded as data outliers. Particularly problematic is that the collaborative teams that meet are complacent about these students' lack of progress, instead attributing lack of progress to individual characteristics.

Yesinia has been charged with leading an effort to build the school's professional learning community. Determined to draw on Mindframe 7, "I engage as much in dialogue as in monologue," she has sought to learn from others. So far, she has visited each collaborative team to observe their meetings, has spoken individually to teacher-leaders and the instructional coach to learn about what is working and what isn't, and has sent an anonymous survey to the teaching staff to get a sense of their beliefs about students and their responsibility to one another. The results of her fact-finding are discouraging but unsurprising: There's little in the way of true collaboration beyond lesson planning happening at the school.

PAUSE AND PONDER

Yesinia will be meeting with the principal to discuss next steps for rebuilding this PLC. What recommendations and actions would you offer Yesinia? Use the mindframes to spark your thinking.

_____

_____

_____

_____

_____

An effective PLC doesn't just happen—it is intentionally built and maintained through continual reinvestment in its well-being. Yet it is surprising how infrequently this occurs. It's more typical that the PLC status is the victim of an unstated assumption that it's business as usual. You know, just like we did last year (and in 2015, and 2005 . . .). That's a big mistake. The first flaw is in believing that groups are static. They're not—they are composed of humans that grow, change, have experiences, and, in the process, alter their own thinking. Even at a school where there has been zero turnover from one year

Module 6: Empower Professional Learning Communities

to the next (and when did that ever happen?), those people are not the same as they were a year ago.

The other flawed assumption is that those who are new to a school simply "know" how your PLC works. Seasoned educators might bring misconceptions about the purpose of a professional learning community based on their past experiences. Furthermore, teachers who are new to the profession are likely to know even less, given that the topic is rarely taught in teacher preparation programs. It's little wonder that the logistics—*what*, *where*, *when*, and *how*—take precedence over the real question: *Why*?

 **A Work in Progress**

THE WHY OF PROFESSIONAL LEARNING COMMUNITIES

What's your *why* when it comes to an effective PLC? Imagine that you're in an elevator with a teacher who is new to your school. In a few sentences, what will you tell them about why a PLC is crucial to the school's success?

_____

_____

_____

WHAT MAKES AN EFFECTIVE PROFESSIONAL LEARNING COMMUNITY?

Hord (2004), a thought leader whose work on PLC dates to the 1970s, investigated and reported on the six characteristics of an effective PLC in 2004:

1. **Structural Conditions:** Time and space to meet.

2. **Supportive Relational Conditions:** Trust and respect across colleagues and ways to discuss challenges in humane and growth-producing ways.

3. **Shared Values and Vision:** Shared beliefs about students and teachers' ability to impact their learning.

4. **Intentional Collective Learning:** Collaborative teams learn from one another.

5. **Peers Supporting Peers:** Teachers observe others inside and outside their grade level or department.

6. **Shared and Supportive Leadership:** Collaborative teams are equipped with the decisional capital to effect change.

 **A Work in Progress**

PROFESSIONAL LEARNING COMMUNITY SELF-ASSESSMENT

Conduct a self-assessment of the current status of your PLC (not individual collaborative teams), using Hord's six characteristics and the rating system below. Where do your strengths lay as a PLC? Where are growth opportunities? Use these descriptions to guide your ratings:

1: This is not yet established in our PLC.

2: This happens randomly and is not commonplace.

3: This exists but couldn't yet be considered systematized.

4: This is systematically embedded within our PLC.

Characteristics of an Effective PLC	Current Rating			
1. **Structural Conditions:** Does our PLC have established times that we are able to meet? Are there schedules that support collaboration and diminish isolation in place? Are needed resources available?	1	2	3	4
Ideas for maintaining or strengthening this characteristic:				
2. **Supportive Relational Conditions:** Is there trust and respect in place within your PLC that provides the basis for giving and accepting feedback to work toward improvement?	1	2	3	4
Ideas for maintaining or strengthening this characteristic:				
3. **Shared Values and Vision:** Do members of the team have the same goal? Do they have shared beliefs about student learning and the ability to impact it?	1	2	3	4
Ideas for maintaining or strengthening this characteristic:				

Characteristics of an Effective PLC	Current Rating			
4. **Intentional Collective Learning:** Does our PLC engage in discourse and reflection around sharing practices, knowledge, and skills to impact the growth and achievement of our students? Do we find ways to learn from each other or learn together?	1	2	3	4
Ideas for maintaining or strengthening this characteristic:				
5. **Peers Supporting Peers:** Does our PLC support lifting each other up? Do we celebrate individual and group successes? Do we observe one another while engaged in practice to help each other strengthen their practice?	1	2	3	4
Ideas for maintaining or strengthening this characteristic:				
6. **Shared and Supportive Leadership:** Are power, authority, and decision making shared and encouraged between teachers and building leaders? Is there a positive relationship between administrators and teachers in the school where all staff members grow professionally as they work toward the same goal?	1	2	3	4
Ideas for maintaining or strengthening this characteristic:				

Source: Fisher et al. (2019).

AN INQUIRY CYCLE TO FOCUS THE WORK

Evidence-informed decision making is central to the work of a PLC and its collaborative teams. The practice of examining data is embedded in the work of most teams, but without an inquiry cycle to bracket their work, collaborative teams risk drifting away from their true purpose, which is formulating solutions and testing them. Instead, they admire the problem for a while and conclude that there is little they can do.

That was the case in a year-long study of the language used by collaborative teams in PLCs (Evans et al., 2019). The researchers were interested in learning how teams discussed the data of low-performing students. Over the course of the year, these collaborative teams utilized data regularly in their discussions. The problem? Most of these discussions (85%) focused on the individual characteristics of the students as the explanation for why the child was not performing at expected levels. Much of it was speculative ("I think he's dyslexic") or focused on the family ("They don't read to her at home"). In other cases, it was attributed to a mismatch between the assessment demands and the student ("He's an English learner, and this is a test they always do poorly on"). A significant portion of their explanations had to do with student behavior ("He doesn't pay attention"). Only 15% of the time did their discussions turn to teaching. The result? These teachers' explanations were disempowering. They simply could not see how any of their actions could influence the outcomes.

Collaborative teams in a PLC benefit from a cycle of inquiry that provides them with a path forward. Our PLC+ work focuses its efforts on moving from examining data to understanding how teachers can use those data to monitor their efforts, make decisions, and learn as a group. The inquiry cycle is driven by five essential questions (Fisher et al., 2019):

Evidence-informed decision making is central to the work of a PLC and its collaborative teams.

1. Where are we going?

2. Where are we now?

3. How do we move learning forward?

4. What did we learn today?

5. Who benefited and who did not benefit?

This iterative inquiry cycle seeks to meld Hord's six characteristics of an effective professional learning community into the work of collaborative teams. While the first two questions invite teams to set goals and examine data, it doesn't end there.

The third question moves teams to examine evidence-based practices in light of their agreed common challenge, a principle central to shared values and vision.

The fourth question reminds us that the "L" in PLC stands for the learning of adults, echoing Hord's reminder that peers need to support peers.

The fifth question keeps issues of structural and institutional inequities front and center and challenges teams to refuse to accept the status quo. In other words, despite Shakespeare's words in *The Tempest*, the past does not have to be prologue. We can control and influence the narrative, provided we have the decision-making capital to do so. In doing so, we enact Mindframe 10: a focus on learning and a contribution to a shared language of learning.

 Working on the Work

INFORMATIONAL REFRAMING

Use an informational reframing protocol to analyze the section "An Inquiry Cycle to Focus the Work." Consider what it is you knew about inquiry cycles as you approached this section. Then consider how the information in this passage was similar to and different from your prior knowledge. Finally, note the inferences you are making about inquiry cycles now and your reframed conclusions.

I already knew these things about PLC inquiry cycles:

Similarities Between the Passage and My Prior Knowledge	Differences Between the Passage and My Prior Knowledge

I can now infer . . .

My reframed conclusions are . . .

THE GOAL OF A PROFESSIONAL LEARNING COMMUNITY

Schools are complex organizations filled with younger and older humans who interact in myriad ways. You didn't need this playbook to tell you that. However, one of your chief goals as a school leader is to empower those humans with the ability to take productive action. That concept was first described by Bandura (1977) as self-efficacy, which is the belief that one can execute an action that will deliver a desired result. It's not confidence, because we can be confident that we will fail. It's not self-esteem, which is a measure of self-worth. Efficacious educators understand that they have influence over their environment and are able to align their motivations and behaviors to attain desired results.

Collective efficacy draws on the beliefs of a group that together they can work to accomplish shared goals. The notion of collective efficacy was first explored in the context of neighborhoods confronting rising crime rates. Those neighborhoods with high levels of collective efficacy banded together to successfully create a safer community. The notion of collective efficacy is measured and fostered in disparate workplace environments such as healthcare, among first responders, and corporations, because it is a key to group performance.

As a field, we talk about collective teacher efficacy (CTE), the belief among a group of teachers that they possess the wherewithal to positively impact student learning. It's not "rah-rah, go team" exhortations. The key word is *wherewithal*. Collaborative teams that utilize an inquiry cycle focus on using data, finding out who benefited from their efforts and who didn't, and then doing something about it. They garner evidence of their impact. Among all the 322 influences on student learning identified by Hattie in the Visible Learning mega meta-analyses, collective teacher efficacy is at the top, with an effect size of 1.36. You read that correctly. CTE has the potential to accelerate learning at a breath-taking level.

However, collective teacher efficacy residing inside of a single collaborative team is not going to deliver breakthrough results. CTE has a multiplicative effect across teams when there is a commitment to sharing successes. A PLC that promotes regular interactions among collaborative teams can capitalize on the learning of others. It allows you to take innovative practices to scale. At the school where two of us work, our PLC hosts two World Cafes each year, at the end of the first and second semesters. Representatives from each collaborative team host simultaneous interactive sessions about their semester of inquiry cycles, their results, and their learning. Teachers move freely to sessions and engage in dialogue about the work. After several rotations, they reconvene as collaborative teams to discuss what they have learned from others, as well as the implications for their future work. (If you'd like to learn more about the World Café method, please visit http://www.theworldcafe.com.)

The point isn't to replicate this singular method but rather to plan for how it is that the PLC learns. Organizational theorist Senge (2012) noted in his book *Schools That Learn*:

> Through learning we re-create ourselves. Through learning we become able to do something we never were able to do. Through learning we reperceive the world and our relationship to it. Through learning we extend our capacity to create, to be part of the generative process of life. (p. 19)

A PLC regularly looks inward to learn about what is working to amplify successes. It also hosts honest conversations about the challenges it faces, with an understanding that the challenge isn't owned solely by one teacher, department, or grade level. A highly effective PLC understands that learning holds the center—not only for the students but for the adults as well.

ALL IN A DAY'S WORK

Consider the questions below and complete the chart to capture your thinking about how to lead your PLC effectively.

Which of your current practices align most strongly with leading an effective PLC?

➡ Place these practices in the KEEP section of the chart.

Which of your current practices are not in alignment with leading an effective PLC?

➡ Place these practices in the STOP section of the chart.

What practices are you considering adding to strengthen your leadership-aligned leading and effective PLC?

➡ Place these practices in the START section of the chart.

ACTIONS	PRACTICES BASED ON MY LEARNING IN THIS MODULE:
KEEP	I will continue to . . .
STOP	I will stop . . .
START	I will start . . .

CONCLUSION

We can't resist using another quote: "The bad leader is he who the people despise; the good leader is he who the people praise; the great leader is he who the people say, 'We did it ourselves'" (Lao Tzu, a sixth-century philosopher). An effective PLC is composed of collaborative teams that learn internally, share their learning with other teams, and, in the process, build their collective efficacy to positively impact student growth. As a member of your PLC, your goal is to empower. As a great leader, it is music to your ears to hear teachers say, "We did it ourselves."

Access resources, tools, and guides
for this module at the companion website:
resources.corwin.com/howleadershipworks

7

ENSURE GROWTH–ORIENTED FEEDBACK

LEARNING INTENTIONS

- I am gaining a clear understanding about feedback as a powerful influence that impacts the learning of all members of the school community.

- I am learning how different types of feedback are required to move learners to deep levels of learning.

SUCCESS CRITERIA

- I can provide a rationale and process for building a feedback culture in the school.

- I can harness the power of feedback that improves learning.

- I can lead discussions using multidirectional feedback in which students, teachers, and leaders give, seek, receive, and act on feedback to and from each other.

- I can leverage the three feedback questions for school improvement:
  - Where are we going?
  - How are we doing?
  - Where to next?

Feedback has long been known as a powerful influence on learning and achievement, and it has long been a challenge for schools to get it right. Teachers typically express confidence that they provide quality feedback to students on a regular basis; however, students report they rarely receive helpful feedback. In addition, trained classroom observers describe low levels of feedback in interactions between teachers and students. Hattie and Yates (2014) describe this challenge as an "empathy gap" because the same event is reported differently based on who you are, the role you occupy, and the nature of the relationship in the interaction.

Feedback has a powerful impact on student learning; according to new research housed at visiblelearningmetax.com, feedback has an effect size of 0.62. This research delineates the findings further by placing types of feedback into various categories, including

➡️ Feedback on tasks and process: 0.62

➡️ Timing of feedback: 0.49

➡️ Feedback involving reinforcements and cues: 0.92

The effect of feedback is among the most variable (Hattie & Clark, 2019), meaning that there are wide differences in the impact that feedback has, from very low to much stronger. In part, this is because some of the feedback isn't very good and in part because some of the feedback never gets in. There is a difference between feedback sent and feedback received.

Nuthall (2007) also notes that most feedback students receive comes from their peers, and it is usually wrong.

In this module, we describe the feedback practices that have the greatest impact on learning. As leaders, Mindframe 6 calls us to foster a culture of feedback where teachers, students, and leaders seek, give, receive, and act on feedback. To do this well, we must first know what works.

A LEADER'S CHALLENGE

Juan is the principal of a struggling middle school located on the fringe of a large metropolitan area. Students who attend school here come from hard-working families who value education. Juan considers himself blessed to serve this community, and he works tirelessly to ensure a "life-altering education" for all his students. Juan strives to find and use educational practices that work best for student learning. Through his research, Juan learned about the powerful impact of feedback. He read books and articles by John Hattie and others and developed a deep understanding of the *what*, *why*, and *how* of quality feedback and the benefits of feedback on student learning.

As he learned about feedback, Juan became acutely aware that his school needed to focus on this powerful practice. As he visited classrooms, he noted that teachers did almost all the talking in class. By his calculations, they talked 90% of the time. He also noted that when feedback was offered to students about their learning, it was done so for the whole class and was void of information on what specific students needed to do next to improve their learning. He observed feedback that was more behavioral than instructional and that included lots of general praise.

When Juan asked students about the feedback they received from the teachers, they indicated it was mostly through grades and that very little of what they get verbally or in writing was helpful. Students indicated they wanted feedback that would help them know what to do next in their work and that they needed to know what they were working toward at the beginning of a unit or lesson.

When Juan talked with teachers about their feedback practices, they spoke confidently about providing feedback to all students. They mentioned the time they dedicated to feedback and their desire to help students move forward in their learning. Juan compared his discussions with teachers and students to his classroom observations and became concerned about the significant gap in what teachers believed they were doing and the actual practices he had observed.

As Juan began to get a clearer picture of how much work they had to do to bring their feedback practices up to speed, he decided that he needed to start by building a feedback culture where teachers, leaders, and students were taught explicitly what feedback is and is not, and how to give, seek, receive, and act on feedback to improve learning. He also needed to work to resolve the gap in perceptions about feedback between teachers and students by building a schoolwide shared understanding. This was Juan's leadership challenge.

PAUSE AND PONDER

Do you have an empathy gap regarding feedback in your school? If you are not sure, conduct some action research. Ask students and teachers about the feedback they give and receive and note any discrepancies between the two. Then compare their responses to what you and your team have observed in classes. What are the results? Is there a shared understanding about feedback throughout the school? If not, consider the information that follows in this module to help close the empathy gap in your school.

FEEDBACK DEFINED

Feedback is generally defined as information allowing a learner to reduce the gap between what is already known and what should be known. Feedback provides information about the next step to be taken. According to Hattie, effective feedback helps someone understand what they know, what they don't know, and where they need to go next. Wiggins (2012) notes that "feedback is information about how we are doing in our efforts to reach a goal. . . . Helpful feedback is goal-referenced; tangible and transparent; actionable; user-friendly (specific and personalized); timely; on-going; and consistent."

Feedback can be expanded to include two-way channels designed to guide learners, whether they are students, teachers, or leaders, as they progress toward their goals. Multidirectional feedback includes not only feedback from teachers to students, but also from students to teachers. It includes feedback from leaders to teachers as well as feedback from teachers to leaders and teachers to teachers. It also includes student-to-student feedback as well as student self-assessment. In this model, feedback flows to and from all members of the school community who have learned how to seek, give, receive, and act on feedback to improve learning for all.

BUILDING A SHARED UNDERSTANDING

Fostering a feedback culture and a shared understanding of feedback can be achieved by communicating the key points Hattie and Yates (2014) offer for effective feedback below. As you read, think about best approaches for sharing this information with your team(s). Each of the key points is supplemented with information to provide clarity, and key points have been edited for length.

- **Feedback is not an isolated process**. Feedback is embedded within a sequence of instructional moves in which teachers convey to students that specific outcomes are attainable. These instructional moves may include modeling and direct instruction, collaborative learning, inquiry, practice, or a host of other approaches. For example, learners can seek and receive feedback as they work collaboratively or as they observe the teacher demonstrate a task. Each instructional move is guided by the learning intentions and success criteria, and feedback is anchored to the criteria. This encourages students to assess where they are and where they are going.

- **Feedback works best when criteria for success are known to the learner in advance**. Feedback based on the criteria for success for a learning intention makes sense to students and provides them with clarity of direction and destination. Students can react to feedback based on success criteria in ways that move them along a learning pathway. This kind of feedback enables students to respond to the three key feedback questions: *Where am I going? How am I doing? Where to next?*

- **Feedback can cue attention to a task when there is a known goal**. Learning intentions and success criteria provide the goals for a learning endeavor and they help to ensure that learning tasks have purpose. When students have clarity about the learning intentions and success criteria, they see the purpose of the tasks and thus will respond to feedback that directs their attention to the tasks.

- **Feedback must engage learners at, or just above, their current level of functioning**. This is what Hattie calls the Goldilocks principle: feedback that is not too hard and not too boring. This requires that teachers know their learners well and know where the sweet spot is between challenging and boring, and provide feedback that moves them just above their current level of functioning.

➡ **Feedback thrives in an environment where errors are welcomed.** Classroom cultures built on trust between teachers and students and among students are environments where errors can be seen as opportunities to learn. In these classrooms, teachers explain the learning process and the role of productive struggle when learning. They reinforce the notion that if mistakes are not being made, nothing new is being learned. Once students experience this kind of environment, they begin to trust that they can expose their mistakes to peers and truly learn from them. This allows teachers to provide feedback challenging students to invest effort in learning hard things.

➡ **Feedback should be evaluated based on what learners receive and interpret.** Teachers typically think of good feedback as the one delivered to students. However, the impact of feedback must be evaluated based on what the learners gain from the feedback and how they interpret and implement it. Feedback is used and received by students when teachers adapt and adjust their methods and set priorities based on student performance. Thus, Hattie advises not to focus on giving more feedback, but rather spend time investigating what students are taking from the feedback given and what they do as a result. When we strive to evaluate our impact on learners, as indicated in Mindframe 1 for both teachers and leaders, we must inquire with the learners about whether the feedback is, and/or is not, working for them.

 ## A Work in Progress

CREATING A SHARED UNDERSTANDING

Below are several key points about effective feedback. For each of the key points, place a checkmark in the column that best reflects where your school currently falls on that practice. The results will help you determine where to start in building a shared understanding and strengthening of effective feedback practices.

Key Points	Affirms	Not Yet	Conflicts
1. Feedback is not an isolated process.			
2. Feedback works best when criteria for success are known to the learner in advance.			
3. Feedback can cue attention to a task when there is a known goal.			
4. Feedback must engage learners at, or just above, their current level of functioning.			
5. Feedback thrives in an environment where errors are welcomed.			
6. Feedback should be evaluated based on what learners receive and interpret.			

On the form below, record the key point(s) that are not yet a common practice in your school and any notes you want to capture to explain why not. Then, record the feedback key points that conflict with your current practices and your thoughts about why this might be. You will return to these notes at the end of the module to help in planning your next/needed steps to strengthen feedback practices for learning.

FEEDBACK KEY POINTS

Not Yet a Common Feedback Practice	Important to Note
1.	
2.	
3.	

Conflicts With Current Feedback Practice(s)	Important to Note
1.	
2.	
3.	

What conclusions are you drawing from the results above? As you work through this module, keep this information in mind.

_____

_____

_____

CREATING FEEDBACK–FRIENDLY CLASSROOMS

As you reflect on the current practices in your school regarding feedback for improved learning, to what extent do you observe explicit teaching about feedback? Furthermore, to what extent do your students understand why feedback is given, how feedback should be given, how learners seek feedback, and/or how learners act on feedback? If your school is like most, you have not yet considered explicit instruction on feedback an essential aspect of your work. Yet we often hear from teachers that students do not use feedback to deepen their learning or improve their performance, nor do they self-assess to regulate their own learning, and it is often said that students are not capable of providing effective feedback to enhance the learning of others. This sentiment could not be more inaccurate.

Hence, one of the most important steps a teacher can take in creating a feedback-friendly classroom is to explicitly teach students about feedback. Teachers can model their feedback-seeking habits by creating posters that make it clear to others that they welcome feedback.

Teachers can also teach students to engage deeply in the feedback process in several ways. Direct instruction on what feedback is, why we give and receive it, and how feedback helps us learn is a great starting point. Another is by providing clarity in learning intentions and success criteria used as the basis for feedback to move learning forward. View the examples below from a multi-grade special needs classroom, and think about how the clarity students are gaining in the learning intentions and success criteria help make the feedback clear and help them see the next step in their learning.

EXAMPLES 1 AND 2

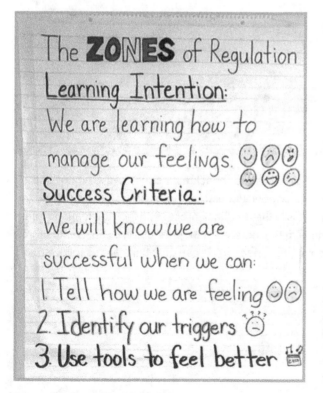

Source: Courtesy of Patricia McGuire

How would clarity, as illustrated in this example, help students understand and receive feedback for learning? Make note of the ideas you are developing to make classrooms in your school more feedback-friendly through greater clarity.

_____

_____

_____

_____

_____

_____

_____

_____

_____

_____

_____

_____

MULTIDIRECTIONAL FEEDBACK IN THE CLASSROOM

Once students learn about and begin to use feedback as a consistent element of their learning routine, they will develop a deeper understanding of how to use the learning intentions and success criteria as tools in the feedback process. In fact, the learning intentions and success criteria are critical to teachers' and students' ability to answer the three feedback questions to guide them in their learning. These questions are as follows:

➡ Where am I going?

➡ How am I doing?

➡ Where to next?

The examples that follow, from a third-grade classroom, can be used to demonstrate how feedback based on clear learning intentions and success criteria can work.

EXAMPLES 3 AND 4

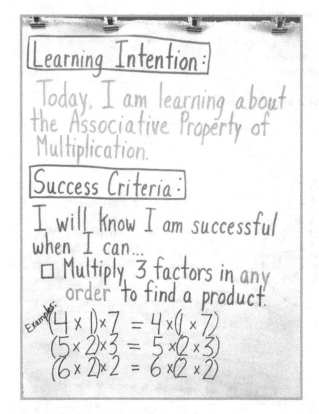

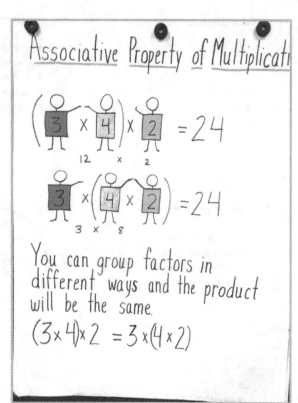

Source: Courtesy of Jeannette Crabtree.

In these math examples, students are learning to use the associative property of multiplication. The teacher has provided worked examples for students to self-assess, and teacher modeling will provide students with clarity on the associative property. As students work to solve the multiplication problems, feedback from the teacher focuses on the various ways associative property can be used successfully. The next learning step will be based on students' ability to group factors in different ways to produce the same product. The teachers' feedback also guides the students in learning how to use the success criteria to monitor their own learning.

Students are able to provide helpful feedback to their peers when they have met and understand the criteria for success. In this context, feedback flows from the teacher to students, from students to students, and from students to the teacher. This is feedback from the students to the teacher and is the most valuable feedback for impacting instruction and the next steps of the teacher.

 Working on the Work

COMPASS POINTS PROTOCOL

As you consider the impact you wish to have on the feedback culture in your school, remember Mindframes 1–3 on monitoring your impact as a leader. These can enable you to create a culture for feedback in your school. Consider exploring the questions in the Compass Point Protocol to capture your thinking. Take notes right on the page. You may want to share these ideas with your team and plan next steps.

_____   **N = Need to Know**   _____
_____   _____
_____   What else do you need to   _____
_____   know about this idea?   _____
_____   What additional   _____
_____   information would help
                               you to evaluate things?

W = Worrisome   **E = Excited**

What do you find   What excites you
worrisome about this   N   about this idea? What
idea or information?   is the upside?
What is the downside?   W   E

                                 S

_____   **S = Stance and Suggestions**   _____
_____   _____
_____   What is your current stance   _____
_____   about this idea or   _____
_____   information?   _____
                               What are your suggestions
                               for moving forward?

Image credit: Photoco/istockphoto.com

MATCHING FEEDBACK TO LEARNERS' INSTRUCTIONAL LEVELS

According to Hattie and Timperley (2007), feedback works best when matched to the student's instructional level, and it should be differentiated according to its level of cognitive complexity. These authors propose four levels or types of feedback referring to a task, a process, one's self-regulation, or oneself.

Self-Level Feedback

At the self level, teachers' feedback involves the personal characteristics of the recipient. Oftentimes, this includes praise, such as being a hard worker or staying focused. It can also contain criticism at the personal or self-level that might include comments such as "always being off task" or "being lazy." This type of feedback contains little information about where the learner is in the learning or what to do next to move forward. Additionally, this type of feedback does not move learners closer to the learning intention and does not teach students how to own their learning or self-regulate it. The following are examples of teacher prompts at the self-regulation level:

→ This work is fabulous!

→ You need to put much more effort into this, John.

In both, the learner has no idea what to do next. Thus, this type of feedback has very little impact on learning.

Task-Level Feedback

At the task level, teachers provide feedback that builds surface-level knowledge, commonly known as *corrective feedback* or *knowledge of results*. It is the most common type of feedback experienced by students, regardless of their instructional level. However, it is limited in its impact on future learning because learners are unable to generalize and apply the feedback in the future. It is most often provided in comments on assignments, and it is often specific rather than generalizable. It is teacher directed and usually involves telling students if they are "right or wrong" and/or specifically what the student needs to do to move forward. Examples include noting "correct or incorrect responses, needing more or different responses, providing more or different information relevant to the task, and building more task knowledge" (Hattie, 2012, pp. 118–119). Teacher prompts to give feedback at the task level:

→ What did the student do well?

→ Is the student's answer correct/incorrect?

→ Where did the student go wrong?

Process-Level Feedback

At the process level, teachers provide feedback aimed at the processes used to create the product or to complete the task. This type of feedback can lead to

→ Alternative processing of tasks

→ Developing or reinforcing learning strategies and error detection approaches

➡️ Cue learners to seek more information and recognize relationships between ideas

➡️ Students using strategies to solve new tasks

Examples include helping to provide connections between ideas, providing strategies for identifying errors, learning how to explicitly learn from mistakes, and providing cues about different strategies or errors. "During process level feedback, the teacher is intending to turn more of the thinking over to the student by guiding them through their own thinking" (Hattie, 2012, p. 119). In doing so, the student has information they can use in future learning situations. Teacher prompts to give feedback at the process level:

➡️ What is wrong and why?

➡️ What strategies did the student use?

➡️ What is the explanation for the correct answer?

➡️ What are the relationships with other parts of the task?

Self-Regulation Level Feedback

At the self-regulation level, teachers focus on building student skills in monitoring their own learning processes. Feedback at this level can enhance students' skills in self-evaluation, provide greater confidence to engage further with the task, and enhance the willingness to invest effort into seeking and dealing with feedback information. Examples include, "helping students to identify feedback themselves and how to self-evaluate, providing opportunities for deliberate practice and effort, and developing confidence to pursue the learning" (Hattie, 2012, p. 120). The following are teacher prompts to give feedback at the self-regulation level:

➡️ How can students monitor their own work?

➡️ How can students carry out self-checking?

➡️ How can students reflect on their own learning?

Finally, Hattie and Timperley (2007) conclude that feedback needs to focus on the appropriate question and level of cognitive complexity; if it does not, the message can easily be ignored, misunderstood, and of low value to the recipient. The level of detail in the feedback and its timing are key to improving the effectiveness for the learner. Hattie says great feedback to learners is just in time, just for me, delivered when and where it can do the most good for learning. Generally, it has been shown that most of the feedback given by teachers is task feedback, the most well-received and interpreted feedback by students is about "where to next," and the least effective feedback is self or praise feedback (Hattie & Timperley, 2007).

 **A Work in Progress**

ANALYZING FEEDBACK OPPORTUNITIES

As you visit classrooms, notice the ways in which feedback is given to students. Use the following tool to determine areas of need based on what you observe in classes.

The feedback was	Rarely	Sometimes	Often
Linked to the learning intentions			
Accurate and trustworthy (with teachers and students in agreement about what counts as success)			
Integrated into the flow of the lesson and provided when students need it to improve learning			
Initiated by students			
Focused on strengths and "where to next," but did not threaten self-esteem			
Directed toward enhanced self-efficacy and more effective self-regulation			
Conversational (either written or oral) rather than one-way			
Used in conjunction with self- and/or peer-assessment			
Actionable with the student given time in which to respond to and act on feedback			
Focused on effort rather than only success			

Source: Adapted from The Education Hub (n.d.).

Which areas are strong in your school or district? Where does effort need to be allocated?

_____

_____

_____

_____

_____

_____

FEEDBACK PRACTICES FOR ADULT LEARNING

Reflect for a moment on the conversation protocol you were provided in Module 2 to guide conversations with teachers following formal and/or informal visits to their classrooms. The protocol is structured to engage both teacher and leader in dialogue about instruction and collaboration and next steps for improvement. The protocol is aligned to the following leadership mindframes:

➡ Mindframe 7: I engage in dialogue more than monologue.

➡ Mindframe 3: I collaborate with teachers about my conceptions of progress and my impact.

➡ Mindframe 1: I am an evaluator of my impact on teacher learning.

To add to this, it is important to note that some feedback that enriches the learning of adults is quite similar to practices that enrich the learning of students, most especially leveraging the three feedback questions. Do adults in schools and districts—teachers, coaches, specialists, paraeducators, etc.—have the clarity needed to answer the questions? Do they know

1. Where they are going?

2. How they are doing?

3. Where to next in their own learning?

They too can benefit from clarity as it relates to the common instructional practices, rituals, and/or routines the leader expects for all staff in the school. These adult success criteria serve as the anchor for feedback that flows from and to teachers and leaders in the school. It provides the foundation for teachers to self-assess and regulate their performance, as well as the benchmarks to monitor their progress toward the desired performance.

Furthermore, the feedback processes for adults should encourage a feedback flow that goes from leaders to teachers, teachers to teachers, and teachers to leaders. How that happens should be consistent and transparent, and the leader models what it looks like when all learners (students, teachers, and leaders) seek, receive, act on, and give feedback to enhance the learning of all.

When these key elements are consistently part of informal and formal feedback conversations, they foster greater trust and receptivity to feedback, thus strengthening the impact of feedback on student learning.

ALL IN A DAY'S WORK

Consider the questions that follow and complete the chart to capture your thinking on strengthening feedback practice to improve learning. Remember to refer to your responses on the key points of feedback completed on page 114.

Which of your common practices were affirmed in the key points assessment?

➡ Place these practices in the KEEP section of the chart.

Which of the feedback key points did you record as conflicts with your common practice(s)?

➡ Place these practices in the STOP section of the chart.

Which of the key points did you record as not yet a common practice?

➡ Place these practices in the START section of the chart.

ACTIONS	PRACTICES BASED ON MY LEARNING IN THIS MODULE:
KEEP	I will continue to . . .
STOP	I will stop . . .
START	I will start . . .

CONCLUSION

In this module, we studied what works best in feedback. We also explored what it means to have a school in which a culture of multidirectional feedback—where all learners seek, give, receive, and act on feedback—is cultivated. We determined that fostering a feedback culture and a shared understanding of feedback can be achieved by communicating the key points offered by Hattie and Yates (2014). These feedback key points include understanding that

- Feedback is not an isolated process.

- Feedback works best when criteria for success are known to the learner, which enables students to respond to the following three key feedback questions: *Where am I going? How am I doing? Where to next?*

- Feedback can cue attention to a task when there is a known goal.

- Feedback must engage learners at, or just above, their current level of functioning. This is what Hattie calls the Goldie Locks principle: feedback that is not too hard and not too boring.

- Feedback thrives in an environment where errors are welcomed.

- Feedback should be evaluated based on what learners receive and interpret.

- Feedback can have different perspectives: feed up, feed back, and feed forward.

Additionally, we provided information on how to create feedback-friendly classrooms by explicitly teaching students about feedback and helping them use the learning intentions and success criteria to monitor their own learning. Matching feedback to students' instructional levels (task, process, and self-regulation) is designed to ultimately develop self-reliant learners. Finally, we touched on the importance of clarity in expectations for adults, as well as opportunities for dialogue and collaboration to guide and support professional learning.

Access resources, tools, and guides
for this module at the companion website:
resources.corwin.com/howleadershipworks

THE WORK AHEAD
LEADING CHANGE

Have you heard the old saying, "Nobody likes change except a wet baby?" Or perhaps, "Change is good. You go first." Do you believe that these are true? If so, can you effectively lead change within your organization? Although change can be hard, and it is in our nature to cling to the familiar, educators know that things need to change if we are to prepare future-proof learners thriving in our society.

To lead the change effectively, you need to believe that change is both necessary and possible and be a leader who embraces Mindframe 4: "I am a change agent, and I believe my role is to improve the learning lives of teachers and students." If not, you might be part of the problem. If you are part of the problem, you may need to carefully consider the ways in which your thinking was shaped and how you can update that thinking so that you confidently engage in change processes.

But all is not lost if you question the possibility of change. As Guskey (2020) taught us, behaviors precede beliefs. In other words, act your way into believing. In this part, we provide you with the tools you will need to effectively manage the changes necessary to occur in your school. This requires more than implementing programs. Yes, some programs or initiatives may be necessary. However, change also requires that we stop doing things that are not working. This is known as de-implementation. In other words, there are times when our change efforts focus on getting people to stop doing things that are not working, and there are times when our efforts focus on implementing effective practices.

In this part, we focus on the following:

- Managing and leading change (Module 8)

- Engaging in de-implementation (Module 9)

- Utilizing implementation science (Module 10)

8

MANAGE AND LEAD CHANGE

LEARNING INTENTIONS

- I am learning how to lead change for school improvement.

SUCCESS CRITERIA

- I can describe the 10 principles of leading school change from the research.

- I can assess my current practices based on the 10 principles and make adjustments for greater success.

- I can provide appropriate support to teachers during three phases of the change process.

- I can prepare for and effectively work through the natural resistance to change as it happens during a change initiative.

Leaders must both manage and lead change. Sometimes, that change is not our choice, as was the case with the transformation coronavirus required of schools, or when the state department of education or the local school board adopts new policies that involve changes in school practices. Other times, the change is planned based on evidence and discussions with various stakeholders, as is the case when new instructional materials are purchased. To be successful in change management, we must

1. Understand change

2. Plan change

3. Implement change

4. Communicate change

Without each of these components, we are not likely to be successful. It begins with understanding change. As Mind Tools notes, understanding change requires that you consider the following:

➡ Why do you need to change?

➡ What are your key objectives?

➡ What will the benefits of the change be to the organization?

➡ How will it impact people positively?

➡ How will it affect the way that people work?

➡ What will people need to do to successfully achieve the change? (Mind Tools, n.d.b.)

With answers to these questions, you're ready to lead the change. Honestly, change management is exciting and allows you to deepen your impact on teaching and learning.

A LEADER'S CHALLENGE

Tonya is an executive director of elementary schools in a large metropolitan district. Her superintendent called a cabinet meeting to discuss the third-grade reading scores just released by the state. Again, this year, the reading scores across the district were abysmal. The cabinet members all agree that the results are not isolated to third-grade instruction—that, in fact, the scores reflect what is happening or is not happening in grades K–2. The superintendent informs Tonya and the other principal supervisors that "something needs to change in K–2." To meet the superintendent's directive, Tonya will need to embrace Mindframe 4: "I am a change agent." This is Tonya's leadership challenge.

Tonya and the other executive director of elementary schools decide to collaborate with the director of curriculum and instruction to determine next steps. They first assess the district's reading curriculum and adopted textbooks in grades K–2 and find that they are well aligned to the state English language arts standards for reading. They also review the district's K–2 reading plan, which includes explicit guidelines on how teachers are to use the mandated daily 2.5 hours of ELA time. They conclude that the issue is not misaligned curriculum or weak planning, but that the issue is instruction. This is where the change needs to occur, but how?

Recognizing that the school is the primary unit of change and that interventions at the implementation level are essential, they develop a plan together to assess the current quality of implementation of the reading plan and use of adopted materials. They craft a walk-through tool based on the requirements in the reading plan and then train an in-house team of qualified observers to investigate the current status of classroom instruction aligned to the requirements in the plan. They look for deep implementation of daily shared reading, guided reading, collaborative learning, word study, and writing, as well as the effective use of the adopted reading resources.

Their investigation reveals that teachers are not yet proficient in the required components of the reading plan, and many are still using the old textbooks. No wonder the scores are flat! The team then decides that they must take personal accountability for the lack of teacher proficiency and put forth a districtwide support plan involving whole district training by grade level, small-group training in schools, coaching to provide model lessons, and importantly, support for principals' learning to better monitor reading instruction in their schools. Importantly, they did not blame the teachers or leaders in the schools. Rather, they evaluated their impact based on evidence related to current levels of understanding of the K–2 curriculum and reading plan. They were exhibiting Mindframes 1–3 on evaluating impact.

PAUSE AND PONDER

Reflect on the leadership challenge above and respond to the following questions:

1. Do you believe Tonya and her colleagues will realize the change they hope to see in K–2 classrooms? Why or why not?

_____

_____

_____

_____

2. If you were the director in this case, what would you do differently to lead effective change?

_____

_____

_____

_____

As you read and interact with the content in this module, check your responses to these questions to see if your suggestions align to the principles of leading change successfully.

PRINCIPLES OF LEADING CHANGE

We have learned a lot about successful school change through numerous studies over the past decades. Unfortunately, in sometimes desperate efforts to do the best for students, leaders focus on the "latest and greatest ideas" whether they complement existing efforts or if there is evidence of impact. The late Richard Elmore said that schools do not resist change; they actually change promiscuously! As leaders, we cannot forget the prerequisites for a successful change to occur and then question why a change is not realizing the outcomes we had hoped for. Although leading change is difficult, adhering to the tried-and-true principles found in research can lead to successful change, and it enables the leaders to be change agents, as described in Mindframe 4.

Working on the Work

ANTICIPATION GUIDE

Are you ready to lead change? For each of the statements about change that follow, mark true or false in the *before reading* column based on your current understanding. After reading about the 10 principles of change, return to this anticipation guide and mark your *after reading* responses. Assess and consider the changes.

Before Reading		Change Statements	After Reading		Notes
True	False		True	False	
		1. An entire organization does not change until every individual changes.			
		2. The most important interventions to facilitate change are structural.			
		3. A differentiated approach to address resistance is necessary to move change work forward.			
		4. Top-down mandates can work quite well in prompting change.			
		5. There are two important dimensions that affect change efforts: physical features and people factors.			

Note: Answers available on p. 145.

There are 10 principles of change (Hall & Hord, 2015) that we can use to understand what happens when people inside organizations are engaged in change.

If change is perceived as a process, as opposed to an event, the pace of change actually quickens.

➡ **Change is learning.** Professional learning is a critical component of the change process. As we learn, we are more likely to implement improved programs, processes, and practices.

➡ **Change is a process, not an event.** Most changes in education take years, depending on the change complexity. However, if change is perceived as a process, as opposed to an event, the pace of change actually quickens. When change agents plan for a process, they are much more strategic and likely to accomplish their goals.

➡ **The school is the primary unit for change.** Districts are important in establishing expectations, organizing resources, and setting course, but changes occur at the site level. Individuals at the site, teachers and leaders, will make or break any change effort, regardless of whether the change is initiated from the inside or the outside.

➡ **Organizations adopt change—individuals implement it.** Successful change begins and ends at the individual level. An entire organization does not change until each member has changed. Another way to say this is that there is an individual aspect to organizational change.

➡ **Interventions are key to the change process success.** The actions (i.e., providing training, checking on progress using informal interviews, or having teachers produce a self-assessment, etc.) are critical to successful change. Interventions come in different sizes. Some important interventions are the little ones, and it is the quantity of the little things that makes the final difference.

➡ **Appropriate interventions reduce the resistance to change.** Leaders must determine the reason for any resistance encountered. What appears to be resistance may be an individual working through the sense of loss for having to stop doing something comfortable. Or resistance could be based on questions about whether the change will really be an improvement. Sometimes, there is resistance simply because change is painful. Each of these examples of resistance has very different underlying reasons. In most situations, addressing the resistance requires attending to individual differences.

➡ **Administrator leadership is essential to long-term change success.** Everyone along the evidence to action continuum has a role to play if change is going to be successful. There is a difference between knowing and doing. Administrators must develop the necessary infrastructure changes and long-term resource supports if the use of an innovation is to be implemented and sustained.

➡ **Facilitating change is a team effort.** Leading effective change requires collaboration. When teachers and others inside the organization share successes and challenges, implementation efforts can be more successful.

➡ **Mandates can work.** Although mandates are traditionally criticized as being ineffective because of their top-down orientation, they can work under the right conditions. Mandates make things a priority and establish the expectation that the innovation will be implemented. The mandate approach fails when the only time the change process is supported is at the initial announcement of the mandate. When the top-down mandate is accompanied by bottom-up support (i.e., continuing communication, ongoing learning, on-site coaching, and time for implementation), change is possible.

The context influences the process of learning and change. There are two important contexts affecting the change efforts of the individual and the organization:

- The physical features, such as the size and arrangement of the facility, and the resources, policies, structures, and schedules that shape the staff's work.

- The people factors, which include the attitudes, beliefs, and values of the individuals involved, as well as the levels of trust, relationships, and norms that guide behavior.

Remember to return to the anticipation guide at the start of this section and complete the activity to assess your learning in this section.

THE PEOPLE FACTORS OF CHANGE

Change is more often resisted when people are unsure of the reason for the change. No one bothers to explain to them the *why*. Frequently, school leaders overlook the importance of thinking through, "What's in it for all school stakeholders?" That is, individuals must believe that it is in their own best interest to do things differently.

How many of us have heard the quip: "If it's not broke, break it and improve anyway"? What a waste of resources. Change should only be pursued when there is a clear goal, be it personal, group, organizational, or societal. There is value in consistency rather than changing to be a part of the latest fad. The latter lowers morale and increases cynicism in the workplace.

However, resistance to important and valid change efforts in schools is to be anticipated, too, and it should be considered a normal part of the change process. It is possible to get beyond it with proper planning and the use of Mindframe 7: engage in dialogue, not monologue. According to Hall and Hord (2015), human attitudes and behavior toward any proposed change develop over the course of the implementation. Fullan (2007) built on Huberman and Miles's work (1984) to suggest that as leaders orchestrate a lasting change, we should probably think of that change as happening in three phases: initiation, implementation, and institutionalization.

1. **Initiation** is the "process that leads up to and includes a decision to adopt or proceed with a change" (Fullan, 2007, p. 69). Resistance to change should be expected in these early stages, but it can certainly emerge at any point along the change journey. During the initiation phase, people confront the *technical* aspects of the change. Their focus is on what they will be required to do differently and whether they have the knowledge and skill to do what is expected of them. This is where Mindframe 9 can make a significant impact on success: "I build relationships and trust to make it

safe to make mistakes and learn from others." Having trust and relationships with staff can lower anxiety and calm the feeling that the change will overwhelm them.

During the initiation phase, teachers need clarity about the purpose, goals, and benefits of the change. They need to consistently hear and see how the work will benefit both staff and students.

2. **Implementation** is the phase of change during which teachers are attempting to successfully make the change but are struggling through the learning process of getting it right. Their continued doubt that they have the skills or knowledge necessary may result in more dramatic resistance and cause them to question the value of the change. They also may begin to note shifts in the roles and responsibilities of staff members. These social aspects are particularly tough to navigate because many people have deep, personal reactions to changing "the way we've always functioned." The technical and the social aspects often feed each other to fuel overt resistance. Mindframe 6 thus can provide guidance here as seeking feedback from staff on how things are going, and what support would be beneficial, can help staff persist through this stage of learning. During implementation, it is important for teachers to experience short-term wins and for leaders to celebrate the progress along the way. Leaders who allow for teacher proficiency to grow organically, while also providing guardrails to keep moving forward, are generally more successful with keeping teachers engaged in the work.

> **During the initiation phase, teachers need clarity about the purpose, goals, and benefits of the change.**

3. **Institutionalization** is when the practice becomes embedded into daily routines in deep and powerful ways. But, if the implementers aren't continually reminded of the purpose of the change and don't receive practical forms of professional learning to deepen their skills, their focus and energy on the work could fade, and resistance could grow. During institutionalization, leaders can support teachers by recognizing that they want to talk about their progress and the concerns they may have. Leaders need to ask and sincerely listen to staff about their continued challenges and develop supports to address them. People tend to stay engaged when they are heard and supported.

Finally, there is no such thing as an instantaneous transformation. Asking people to change without giving them reasons and resources to do so is counterproductive. "Turning the organization on a dime" or "pulling the organization through a knothole" are metaphors that do no justice to the process of change. Change involves time and the opportunity to learn, and learning is often inefficient. So don't expect the performance to improve too quickly.

Leaders serving as effective change agents should understand the phases of change and how to navigate through them successfully. Resistance to change is predictable, but leaders can plan for success by supporting staff through the technical and social aspects of the change process. This requires that the leader closely observe the behavior of team members and listen to what they are saying. Then, we must match our support to the challenges they are working through.

COMMUNICATING CHANGE

Hiatt and colleagues (2006) studied more than 700 organizations and noted that communications regarding change were one of the reasons that efforts failed. Based on their investigations, they developed the ADKAR components: **awareness** of the need for change, **desire** to participate in and support it, **knowledge** of how to change, **ability** to change, and **reinforcement** to sustain the change in the long term.

This model allows leaders to identify areas of resistance and increase communication so that all stakeholders understand the reasons for the change and what is required. For example, if someone is unable to change because they do not understand why change needs to happen, support would be provided at the awareness level. If someone does not understand how to make a change, you may consider knowledge building.

Awareness. When the leader can communicate about each of the five components of ADKAR, there is an increased likelihood that change will occur. Let's re-consider Tonya's experience with the reading scores. To create the change within the school system, Tonya and her team would need to be clear about why there was a need to change. It's not enough to simply announce the change. People need to understand the reasoning behind the change and come to agree with that reasoning. Skilled change leaders can articulate the need for the change, answer questions about the change, and focus on the benefits to others of implementing the change. Team members should be encouraged to ask why questions about the change so that their awareness is increased.

> **People need to understand the reasoning behind the change and come to agree with that reasoning.**

Desire. Leaders foster a desire to change. One way to do this is to identify change leaders, or early adopters. These people demonstrate public support for the change and can share benefits related to implementing the change. They can also answer questions from their peers and provide examples of how they enacted the change. Leaders can also foster a desire to change when they are passionate about the benefits to students and staff.

Knowledge. Understanding that there is a need for change and knowing what to do are two different things. This is where new learning enters the picture. Effective leaders make it clear that they are on a learning journey and that people are not expected to already know everything. It's best practice to conduct a needs assessment so you know what knowledge people need to be successful. As part of the knowledge building, people need to know how their responsibilities, skills, and processes will be impacted, and this calls for the leader to have clarity about the change, how all the parts work together, and the impact on each team member.

Ability. When it comes to ability, there is a difference between knowing how to do something and having the confidence to do it. Nancy watches a lot of football and has considerable knowledge of the game. But she does not have the confidence or will to actually play it. In this case, there's nothing wrong with that. However, educators need to develop their confidence and the will to implement change, and that happens with their leader's support. Often, educators need some time to engage in safe practice, without fear of being observed, so that they can try one of the changes. Without opportunities for safe practice, teachers tend to use reliable approaches rather than innovate because they are concerned that they might fail or look bad on early attempts in implementation.

Reinforcement. It's important that leaders reinforce the incremental changes that they see. When success approximations are reinforced, lasting change is more likely. Leaders should recognize and celebrate the success of their team members, and it's okay to do so in a public way. However, we should correct mistakes, or slip into old habits, in private. As part of the reinforcement phase, leaders continue to collect information to determine whether the change has been implemented, as well as when and where additional supports may need to be provided.

Heifetz and Linksy (2002) offer the following metaphor for change leaders: Leaders have to move back and forth from the balcony to the dance floor, over and over again, to maintain an accurate view of how the change initiative is working or not working. Taking the balcony view allows a leader to take a step back and see the big picture, while being on the dance floor enables the change agents to participate in the work with staff as the work unfolds. As the metaphor goes, leaders often return to the balcony from the dance floor to take another look at the big picture. It's the back and forth, from balcony to dance floor, that allows leaders to create change. Sustaining strong change leadership requires first and foremost the capacity to see what is happening to you and your initiative as it is happening and to understand how today's turns in the road will affect tomorrow's plans.

 A Work in Progress

CHANGE INITIATIVE PLANNING

Consider a change initiative that you have experienced or are planning. Use the ADKAR components to plan your communication strategy.

Component	Talking Points
Awareness (of the need for change)	
Desire (to participate in and support it)	
Knowledge (of how to change)	
Ability (to change)	
Reinforcement (to sustain the change in the long term)	

〉〉〉 Working on the Work

CONNECT–EXTEND–CHALLENGE

Reflect on the change projects you have been a part of and complete the following exercise.

What did you discover in your reading in this module that connected to what you already knew about school change?
What did you learn about school change in the reading that extended your understanding with new information?
What did you take from your reading that challenged your thinking about school change?
What will you specifically take from your reading and use to strengthen your next school change initiative?

LEADING CHANGE: REALITY CHECK

To get started on a successful school change project, leaders should conduct a reality check. You must ask yourself:

➡ What initiatives are underway in our school right now?

➡ When was the last time, if ever, that you took an inventory of these initiatives?

➡ How have you measured the impact of the initiatives?

➡ Have you researched to find more effective and impactful practices that can replace those that have not yielded expected results?

Before a change begins, we must understand where we are now.

We suggest conducting an initiative inventory to gain the clarity necessary to effectively lead change. The purpose of the initiative inventory, according to the National Implementation Research Network (NIRN), is to guide the school or district in a review of past and current initiatives to produce a clear picture of existing initiatives, mandates, and resource commitments. Information and data collected can be used to explore the fit of additional initiatives with current work, guide decision making, and assist with alignment of efforts (NIRN, 2020).

Before beginning the inventory, there are a few considerations to note to ensure a smooth and meaningful process. These considerations for schools and districts have been adapted from the NIRN process for state departments of education.

Prerequisites

The following actions are recommended before starting the initiative inventory process.

➡ Share the purpose and process of the inventory with the leadership team. Respond to questions and provide examples.

➡ Develop a clear plan of who will lead the process, key roles needed, process for collecting inventory information, how the information will be used (e.g., intended outcomes), and how it will be embedded into ongoing implementation planning.

Process Coordination

Identify the implementation team members who will coordinate and lead the initiative inventory process. These two or three individuals should ensure that

➡ The plan is developed and executed.

➡ The information collected is used for decision making.

➡ The full implementation team and leadership have regular updates.

➡ A process has been established to maintain and monitor information collected.

Identify Intended Outcomes of the Inventory

Identifying clear purposes and outcomes for the initiative inventory will help the team develop a plan to complete the inventory, maintain the information, and use it to focus future change project work. For example, the inventory initially may be conducted within a specific area (e.g., academic vocabulary) or target a specific group of students (e.g., English learners who have not made a year's worth of progress in the past year) and then later be broadened to include other areas as needed.

Roles Needed During the Process

There are several roles that need to be considered for an initiative inventory to be successful, including

➡ **Facilitator** to guide the discussion among the leadership team members, and potentially staff members, with needed historical information

➡ **Note-taker** to record and distribute minutes to the team

➡ **Technology leader** to create shared documents and files for the team

Guiding Questions to Develop the Inventory

➡ Who is providing leadership for the initiative? Is there a team supporting the initiative? If so, who are the members?

➡ What are the expected outcomes when the initiative is implemented, or what change is expected to occur because of the initiative?

➡ Who is the initiative meant to help (i.e., target population or area)?

➡ Is there a requirement to implement this initiative or report its impact and use? If yes, identify the entity (e.g., state, federal, or other) requiring the initiative.

➡ What are the fiscal resources needed to implement the initiative, or what is the total budgeted amount for this work?

➡ What human resources are required to support the initiative's implementation (e.g., number of full-time equivalents, training needs, technology supports)?

➡ How well aligned is the initiative with your strategic plan?

➡ What data do you have to measure the success or impact of the initiative on intended outcomes?

➡ What impact has the initiative had on its intended outcomes? What is the source of evidence?

You can use the following tool to organize the team and record how the work will get done.

SAMPLE INITIATIVE INVENTORY PROCESS ORGANIZATION TABLE

Initiative Inventory Coordinators	Name	Position

Purpose of Inventory and Desired Outcomes	

Other Roles	Name	Position
Facilitator:		
Note-Taker:		
Technology Leader:		
Respondents:		

Target Dates:	Completion of Inventory	Use of Inventory

Actions Needed	By Whom	By When	Resources Needed

Source: National Implementation Research Network (2020).

Have you ever heard someone say that the new initiative is "just one more thing"? If so, they are probably not seeing the connection between the new, or next, initiative and all the other efforts within the system. Or they may be suffering from "initiative fatigue," which happens when the number of initiatives continues to grow, whereas time, resources, and professional capital are constant. This drains energy and interest in engaging in anything new or different. Before starting something new, it's wise to conduct an initiative inventory so that there is clarity about what already exists, how resources (fiscal, human, physical) are being used, and if this new program complements or conflicts with existing programs. Conducting an initiative inventory allows the team to identify

➡ The number of initiatives (and too many will cause fatigue)

➡ Who is, and is not, benefiting from those initiatives

➡ The adequacy of funding and resources

➡ The effectiveness and outcomes of the various efforts already underway

Sometimes called a horizon scan, this process allows the team to understand the current implementation landscape and to identify commonalities that appear across initiatives that may support or sabotage effective implementation.

After the completion of the inventory implementation on the facing page, team members analyze the results and weigh the benefits of each. Discussions might include evidence for the return on the investment of the initiatives, the alignment and cohesion of the initiatives, the viability of the initiatives in current times, and the research base that currently does or does not support continuing certain initiatives. It is important to keep the inventory current as new change projects and initiatives are brought in. This will make decision making more effective, evidence based, and cost efficient.

A Work in Progress

INITIATIVE INVENTORY SAMPLE TEMPLATE

Review the template below as a way to capture this information and assess the current reality in your school.

Understanding the Implementation Landscape

Team Members: _____   **Date:** _____

Name of Initiative	Leadership of Initiative (Team and/or Coordinator Name(s) and Department)	Expected Outcome	Target Population	Start and End Date	Financial Commitment and Source of Funding (federal, state, grant, or other)	Relation to Organization Priorities and Strategic Plan	Evidence of Outcomes What has happened thus far?

Source: National Implementation Research Network (2017).

ALL IN A DAY'S WORK

Consider the questions that follow and complete the chart to capture your thinking on successfully leading change. Refer to the exercises you completed to inform your responses.

Which of your current practices were affirmed in this module?

→   Place these practices in the KEEP section of the chart.

Which of your current practices conflict with what you have learned in this module?

→   Place these practices in the STOP section of the chart.

What have you learned in this module that will strengthen your practices to successfully lead change?

→   Place these practices in the START section of the chart

ACTIONS	PRACTICES BASED ON MY LEARNING IN THIS MODULE:
KEEP	I will continue to . . .
STOP	I will stop . . .
START	I will start . . .

CONCLUSION

As we noted at the outset of this module, managing and leading change are important aspects of leadership. If leaders are to truly realize school improvement, they must support educators in becoming comfortable with change, as improvement is impossible without change. Great leaders recognize that they must involve people in the collective efforts to improve the schooling experience and provide the supports that would allow them to grow into the change.

In Modules 9 and 10, you will dive deeper into successfully leading change by exploring how your initiative inventory can be used to guide the de-implementation of current initiatives not yielding desired outcomes and impact your implementation process for newly selected projects to yield more desirable outcomes.

*Answer key to the anticipation guide: (1) True, (2) False, (3) True, (4) False, (5) True

Access resources, tools, and guides
for this module at the companion website:
resources.corwin.com/howleadershipworks

9

ENGAGE IN DE-IMPLEMENTATION

LEARNING INTENTIONS

- I am learning about the components of de-implementation planning to increase success on change initiatives.

SUCCESS CRITERIA

- I can explain key underpinnings of a de-implementation process.
- I can connect de-implementation processes to implementation planning.
- I can use my initiative inventory as a de-implementation tool.
- I can differentiate between four types of de-implementation and decide when it is best to use them.
- I can create a draft plan for a change challenge in my school.

More than likely, the term *de-implementation* is a new one for you. It is a term not widely used in education, although it is picking up steam. Educators agree, however, that some form or process of taking things off the plate to create space for new change initiatives is long overdue. How many times have you heard educators say, "My plate is already full and now *they* want me to do *this*?" Responding that they should get another plate is probably not wise. Furthermore, note that the person uses "they," which indicates that the change is not yet accepted. In those cases, you may want to review the section in the previous module about communicating change initiatives.

If we want to derive the greatest benefit from new change initiatives, then we must dive deeply into what we will stop doing and how to stop doing it. We should make these decisions based on the evidence collected to date. The de-implementation process can free up time, energy, and intellectual capital to successfully implement more effective

If we want to derive the greatest benefit from new change initiatives, then we must dive deeply into what we will stop doing.

practices for school improvement. At its core, de-implementation is a change process relying on the initiative inventory you completed in Module 8, followed by sound decision making on what to stop and how to de-implement. De-implementation is closely connected to implementation and should be considered a process, not an event.

A LEADER'S CHALLENGE

Gene is an assistant principal in charge of discipline in a large suburban high school. The community is supportive of the school, and parents move into the school's attendance zone so that their children can attend there. Parents and community members are proud that they have school resource officers to keep the school safe and that they employ a highly qualified and committed teaching staff to provide quality instruction.

But Gene has a concern. There is a disparity in the discipline data indicating that certain groups of students are being punished more harshly than others for seemingly similar offenses. This disparity in discipline is a complex one in this school setting, but Gene and his principal decided that it was of serious concern because it affected student well-being, connectedness to school, academic achievement, and a host of other socio-emotional issues. Addressing this equity gap will rely on Gene's impact as a change agent, as stated in Mindframe 4, and it will be his leadership challenge.

With the support and guidance of his principal, Gene begins an investigation into alternatives to the zero-tolerance policy they have in place. He is looking for a practice or program that can effectively address the discipline gap, keep students in school, create a more welcoming and student-centered culture, and maintain a safe school environment. Gene makes a presentation to the school leadership team on transforming the school from a zero-tolerance punishment-driven system to one relying on restorative practices that are learning driven and student centered.

After seeing the data and recognizing the severe impact suspensions are having on students of color, the team agrees with Gene. After all, the effect size of suspending students is –0.20 (minus, meaning it harms learning). They start by first planning what they will specifically stop doing, rather than simply diving into what they will start doing. The team notes which aspects of the current system are required by the district and how the restorative justice process can replace past ineffective practice. Interestingly, they also spend a good bit of time creating a plan for unlearning. The plan addresses what teachers, counselors, resource officers, students, and parents need to unlearn from past practice to understand and implement the new process.

The team also refers to their initiative inventory to determine whether restorative practices conflict with other initiatives and where they will add value. They look for potential funding sources within the inventory as well. The team is clear that the staff will need support, information, and evidence to make this transition. Thus, it schedules a series of planning meetings, establishes roles and responsibilities, and appoints a technology lead to develop planning templates and maintain a dedicated communications hub for the implementation team. In their future meetings, the team will develop a communication plan, a professional development plan, a coaching plan, and a plan to respond to the challenges and resistance along the way.

PAUSE AND PONDER

Reflect on the leadership challenge above and respond to the following questions:

1. Do you have equity gaps in your school similar to Gene's challenge?

2. What did you notice about the team's approach in considering a change in practice?

3. What would you do if you were Gene?

THE UNDERPINNINGS OF SUCCESSFUL DE-IMPLEMENTATION

According to the de-implementation guide created for the Northern Territory Department of Education in Canada (Northern Territory Government, 2020), there are several foundational underpinnings of a successful process that need to be in place from the start of the initiative. These underpinnings include

➡ Treating de-implementation as a process

➡ Engaging leadership teams throughout the process

➡ Creating a school climate supportive of the notion of de-implementation

Making snap decisions to implement or de-implement an initiative without data and evidence leads to a patchwork of efforts that are rarely coordinated. That is, we jump from one issue to another, putting temporary fixes on problems that just circulate back around to be addressed again. Or we try to implement every shiny new thing every time a new book or article comes out. This causes staff a good deal of anxiety and confusion and diverts energy from getting meaningful work done. A high-quality process, one that is transparent and consistently followed, values the voices of various stakeholders and encourages a strong sense of self in those involved in the decisions, often costs little, and generates long-term sustainable outcomes.

A critical determinant of de-implementation and implementation success is engaged leadership. School leaders play an important role in improving education practices as they actively support and manage the overall planning, resourcing, delivery, monitoring, and refining of the de-implementation and implementation processes. Although principals may be the most relevant leaders in implementation efforts, coaches, assistant principals, and leadership teams who may be closer to such efforts are also essential leaders of the work. Special training or other supports can be used to help leaders at multiple levels in schools and related organizations support de-implementation/implementation by contributing to a positive implementation climate in the school. Central office leaders can be invaluable in the process as they can work with school leaders, provide resources and guidance, help make connections to current district initiatives, and serve as a critical friend as plans progress.

Finally, successful de-implementation and implementation efforts are underpinned by a school climate conducive to change. These efforts are easier when staff members

➡ Feel trusted to try new things and make mistakes (Mindframe 9)

➡ Believe they will be supported with high-quality resources, training, and encouragement to try again and keep improving

➡ Have clarity in the goals and purpose of the change practices they are working hard to master (Mindframe 3)

In such supportive contexts, leaders at all levels develop a sense of enthusiasm, trust, and openness to change. A culture supportive of de-implementation and implementation processes is strengthened when there is shared leadership that explicitly creates opportunities for staff to take on implementation responsibilities. One way to achieve this is to create implementation teams networked to other teams to flatten the organization and improve two-way communications during de-implementation and implementation efforts.

 ## Working on the Work

THE UNDERPINNINGS OF SUCCESSFUL DE-IMPLEMENTATION: KEY WORDS AND FIVE-WORD SUMMARY

For each of the sections that follow, record the key words that resonate with you from the above reading. Then, in the last section, take these key words and create a five-word summary that conveys the key message of the three sections combined.

Follow an established process:
Engage leaders at all levels:
Create a school climate receptive to change:
Five-word summary for this section:

TYPES OF DE-IMPLEMENTATION

There are four types of change that should be considered during de-implementation planning (Northern Territory Government, 2020; Wang, 2018): *reverse, reduce, replace,* and *rethink*. The chart on the next page provides suggestions for when to use each type of change followed by examples, actions, and considerations. It also contains references to learning and unlearning. Learning refers to the process of acquiring new skills or knowledge. Unlearning is a process of discarding outdated mental models to make room for alternative models (Wang, 2018). This information can provide essential clarity during de-implementation discussions as the team charts the path forward on a change initiative.

WHEN TO USE THE FOUR TYPES OF DE-IMPLEMENTATION*

Type	When to Use	Example
Reverse	It is not working anywhere.	**Example:** An instructional practice widely used is evaluated and has shown insignificant or no impact on student outcomes. **Action:** Support staff to unlearn the instructional practice and create understanding about its lack of effectiveness. **Consideration:** The reversal of a practice may require something to take its place so that teachers have appropriate support. See: Replace.
Reduce	It is working in some schools but not all, or for some sub-groups, but not all.	**Example:** An intervention to improve well-being is showing improvements in urban schools, but no improvements have been observed in remote schools. **Action:** The intervention is delivered only to students in urban schools, and students in remote schools are removed from the intervention. Staff who do not work with students in remote schools should be supported to unlearn. See: Reverse. **Consideration:** It may be the case that there is another intervention that will be effective for students in remote schools. See: Replace.
Replace	It is not working, but the problem that it is aiming to improve still exists.	**Example:** An initiative to build English language competence in newly arrived students is not having the desired results, and there remains a large proportion of students who require greater understanding of English to access other areas of the curriculum. **Action:** Identify an alternative approach or initiative shown to be more effective in building English language competence, or an alternative that is evidence informed and make plans to evaluate it. **Consideration:** There may be occasions when an initiative is seen to be effective, but there is an alternative approach that demonstrates greater effectiveness, and under these circumstances, it should still be considered for replacement.
Rethink	It is not working, or has done its job, and should now be de-implemented to make room for something else.	**Example:** A program was designed to improve financial management for small schools in response to a significant number of these schools moving into an unsustainable financial position. Budgets have since improved and are stable, with improvements attributed to the processes and support provided to build capability. **Action:** Consider learning and unlearning for staff, as well as how resources that had been used might be re-distributed to enable a new initiative to grow. **Consideration:** Think about the impact of removing support and strategies to sustain the improvement in financial management given staff turnover. Monitor.

*Adapted from Wang et al. (2018).

Source: Northern Territory Government (2020).

››› Working on the Work

REFLECTION AND PLANNING

Think back to the leader's challenge at the beginning of this module. Refer to the preceding chart to help you answer the following questions:

1. What was the de-implementation response to the equity issue highlighted?

_____

_____

2. Did the team consider the learning and unlearning needed to move forward?

_____

_____

3. What other essential tasks did the team engage in to move from de-implementation to implementation?

_____

_____

Now, move your thinking to a challenge or change you may be facing and refer to the initiative inventory you may have completed after Module 8. Read through the de-implementation types on the facing page again and find one or more that make the most sense for your issue. Understand that you may need to draw on more than one type of de-implementation, as these types are not completely distinct and separate.

My change/challenge is:
The type of de-implementation that is needed is:
The learning and/or unlearning that is necessary is:
The outcomes I anticipate as a result of the change include:

PLAN FOR DE–IMPLEMENTATION

Once you have a clear decision on the practice or program to de-implement, it is time to develop a plan. The Northern Territory Department of Education *De-Implementation Guide* provides a tool to guide planning and offers sample completed plans for your review. The format they suggest follows:

TEMPLATE FOR DE-IMPLEMENTATION PLANNING

Problem	De-Implementation Description	De-Implementation Activities	De-Implementation Outcomes	Outcomes
Why was the initiative implemented? What is the current situation?	What are the active ingredients of your plan?	What blend of activities is needed to support staff, including learning and unlearning?	How will you know the selected type of de-implementation is occurring? Do staff feel the de-implementation is feasible and useful? Short Term	How will students, staff, and the school benefit?
What considerations are needed when making a de-implementation decision?	What activities and behaviors will you see when successful de-implementation occurs?	How will we sustain efforts toward the de-implementation?	Longer Term	

Source: Northern Territory Government (2020).

Review the worked example on the next page to provide clarity on how you might respond to each of the questions in the template.

Problem	De-Implementation Description	De-Implementation Activities	De-Implementation Outcomes	Outcome
Why was the initiative implemented? What is the current situation? An instructional practice widely used is evaluated and has shown insignificant or no impact on student outcomes. **What considerations are needed when making a de-implementation decision?** The reversal of a practice may require something to take its place so that teachers have appropriate support.	**What are the active ingredients of your plan?** Develop a communication strategy to explain to stakeholders why the instructional practice is being reversed and the implications of that reversal. Support staff to unlearn the instructional practice and create understanding about its lack of effectiveness. Alter policies that have led to the instructional practice being implemented and sustained. **What activities and behaviors will you see when successful de-implementation occurs?** Monitor the reversal of the instructional practice.	**What blend of activities is needed to support staff, including learning and unlearning?** Initial staff meetings focus on the evaluation of the instructional practice and give leaders an opportunity to test acceptability. Professional learning and follow-up coaching for staff targeted to eliminate the use of the ineffective instructional practice. Teachers are supported to re-establish timetables for learning that capitalize on the increased time that can be dedicated to effective approaches. Tailored communication to staff, families, and students about the discontinuation of the practice with avenues for feedback. **How will we sustain efforts toward the de-implementation?** Monitor the reversal of the instructional practice through classroom observations—noting the frequency of the practice and any unintended consequences on student outcomes.	**How will you know the selected type of de-implementation is occurring?** **Do staff feel the de-implementation is feasible and useful?** **Short Term** Staff and other stakeholders signal increasing acceptability when surveyed at regular intervals. Teachers report less engagement with the model of instruction. **Longer Term** Classroom observations highlight that the model of instruction is not being used in classrooms. Teachers report that they can spend more time on other more effective approaches.	**How will students, staff, and the school benefit?** The reversal of the ineffective model of instruction will enable teachers to expand the time spent on more effective activities that are currently being compressed. Teachers will be able to focus on the approaches that relate to positive outcomes, students will have exposure to more effective teaching, and outcomes will improve.

Source: Northern Territory Government (2020).

 A Work in Progress

STOP AND JOT

Using the blank template included here, jot down your thoughts on a plan you are considering. The purpose of this exercise is to give you a feel for how the template may help organize your thinking around de-implementation. Consult the worked example for ideas to answer each question. Upon completion of the stop and jot exercise, respond to the following questions:

1. How might this plan template help focus on your change project?

2. How might your leadership team and staff respond to a de-implementation process?

3. What information or data might you need to make a case for using a de-implementation process with all change initiatives?

TEMPLATE FOR DE-IMPLEMENTATION PLANNING

Problem	De-Implementation Description	De-Implementation Activities	De-Implementation Outcomes	Outcome
Why was the initiative implemented? What is the current situation?	What are the active ingredients of your plan?	What blend of activities is needed to support staff, including learning and unlearning?	How will you know the selected type of de-implementation is occurring? Do staff feel the de-implementation is feasible and useful? **Short Term**	How will students, staff, and the school benefit?
What considerations are needed when making a de-implementation decision?	What activities and behaviors will you see when successful de-implementation occurs?	How will we sustain efforts toward the de-implementation?	**Longer Term**	

Source: Northern Territory Government (2020).

ALL IN A DAY'S WORK

Consider the questions that follow and complete the chart to capture your thinking on utilizing a de-implementation process in your school or district. Refer to the exercises you completed to inform your responses.

Which of your current practices were affirmed in this module?

➡ Place these practices in the KEEP section of the chart.

Which of your current practices conflict with what you have learned in this module?

➡ Place these practices in the STOP section of the chart.

What have you learned about de-implementation that will strengthen your effectiveness in leading a change initiative?

➡ Place these practices in the START section of the chart.

ACTIONS	PRACTICES BASED ON MY LEARNING IN THIS MODULE:
KEEP	I will continue to . . .
STOP	I will stop . . .
START	I will start . . .

CONCLUSION

De-implementation is an essential step in the change process, and it is high time school leaders treat it as such. Once a change initiative is introduced and reaches some level of institutionalization as mentioned in Module 8, it is often a struggle to convince people to give it up when it fails to yield results or when it has served its original purpose and is no longer needed. A way to address this reluctance to move on to more effective practices is to utilize a consistent process for taking things off the plate, that is, de-implement them. A process that is transparent and well-understood by everyone in the school is more likely to work. As noted in the introduction, the only way to achieve maximum benefits from the practices we implement is to dive deeply into what we will stop doing, and how to stop doing it, based on evidence of impact, thus freeing up time, energy, and intellectual capital to successfully implement more effective practices for school improvement.

Access resources, tools, and guides
for this module at the companion website:
resources.corwin.com/howleadershipworks

10

UTILIZE IMPLEMENTATION SCIENCE

LEARNING INTENTIONS

- I am learning about sound implementation processes to result in deep implementation of change projects in my school.

SUCCESS CRITERIA

- I can explain implementation science in education.

- I can describe and apply the common themes in implementation frameworks.

- I can discuss the stages of implementation and assess the extent to which they are currently used in my school.

- I can become a change agent (Mindframe 4) by connecting the initiative inventory, de-implementation process, and implementation planning for change initiatives in the future.

In Modules 8 and 9, we discussed the critical first steps to successfully lead change. In Module 8, we discussed the principles of change and creating an initiative inventory as a guide to better decisions about the practices and programs used in your school. Then, in Module 9, we explained the next step in the change process. The idea of de-implementation before implementation is a relatively new approach in education. Although the term itself may be unfamiliar, the concept of taking projects, practices, or programs off the plate before putting something new on the plate is not foreign at all. It is important to engage in de-implementation work before planning for the implementation of a new program or practice.

Educational leaders understand that implementation is a key aspect of what schools do to improve, and yet, it is a domain of school practice that rarely receives sufficient attention. Leaders must pay attention to implementation! Sadly, change ideas are often introduced with little attention to how the changes will be managed and what specific steps are necessary for deep and sustained implementation. Oftentimes the *who, why, where, when,* and *how* are overlooked, meaning implementation risks becoming an add-on task expected to be tackled on top of the everyday work. Even with the best of planning in place, a plethora of obstacles and barriers can develop, making it more difficult to achieve deep implementation of a change (e.g., loss of funding, changes in staffing, changes in leadership at the district office, unforeseen events that require immediate attention such as coronavirus, to name a few). As a result, projects initiated with the best of intentions may "die on the vine" because of too many competing priorities (Education Endowment Foundation [EEE], 2018).

> **Implementation risks becoming an add-on task expected to be tackled on top of the everyday work.**

A LEADER'S CHALLENGE

Sayoko is the new executive director of middle schools in a diverse school district serving 50,000+ students. She is responsible for supervising the principals of the 10 middle schools and is held accountable for student achievement, attendance, discipline, safety, and other outcomes from the 10 middle schools. She serves on the superintendent's cabinet, where the various data points are reviewed and discussed quarterly.

Sayoko has learned much about the current status of each of the middle schools over the past 6 months. She has noted serious equity concerns from her reviews of the overall district middle school data and individual school data. In her visits to the schools, Sayoko has observed the data in play in the daily school operations as well. For example, she notes disproportionality in special education identification and over-identification of certain student groups for self-contained classes.

Additionally, she has become concerned that a majority of students in "general level" classes are students from historically marginalized groups. Of course, she understands this means some students are being underserved; they will have less access to AP and IP programs at the high school and will receive fewer academic diplomas. This will then result in students with potential for rigorous academic work facing challenges gaining access to the nation's best colleges and universities. This is Sayoko's leadership challenge.

At the most recent cabinet meeting, Sayoko made a presentation to the team, illustrating the disparities in gifted identification, special education identification, course scheduling, discipline referrals, and school attendance. She believes that many factors are impacting these outcomes. However, she also feels that eliminating the tracking system is required to level the playing field and equalize access to the high school equivalent courses (e.g., Spanish, Algebra) that are part of the middle schools' offerings.

Sayoko realizes that this will be a battle in some communities. She intends to utilize the available implementation science to create a plan that can steady the ship during the challenges that may lie ahead. She has also researched how to create readiness for change among the staff and parent groups, given the hot-button nature of this issue. Finally, she acknowledges to the team that the decision to de-track the middle schools has little support in the Visible Learning research. De-tracking has a 0.09 effect size, and tracking a 0.10 effect size. In other words, neither option increases learning in significant ways. The ambiguity in the findings also creates an additional leadership dilemma she will have to think through.

PAUSE AND PONDER

Reflect on the leadership challenge above and respond to the following questions:

1. List some of the challenges that Sayoko must anticipate to lead successful change.

_____

_____

_____

_____

2. What suggestions would you make to the team to support more diverse enrollment in the high school course options that will remain in the middle schools?

_____

_____

_____

3. What practices would you suggest to Sayoko and the team to decrease the disproportionality in special education identifications?

_____

_____

_____

_____

IMPLEMENTATION SCIENCE

You may recall that in Module 9, we outlined the essential underpinnings of de-implementation and implementation efforts. These included three essential components. They appear below as a reminder:

1. Approach de-implementation/implementation as a process

2. Engage leaders at all levels throughout the process

3. Create a change-friendly school culture

Successfully adopting new programs and practices requires intentional efforts to change professional practice.

These underpinnings are critical to the implementation process. In addition to the underpinnings, leaders must understand the *science of implementation* to improve the likelihood of success. Implementation science can help change leaders maximize their efforts to improve teaching and learning by providing strategies to ensure that initiatives are actually implemented. Successfully adopting new programs and practices requires intentional efforts to change professional practice. Furthermore, it requires flexibility along the way, as well as sustained efforts to see it through to deep implementation.

There are about 60 implementation frameworks available, and five of these have been used in schools. According to Lyon (n.d.), these frameworks articulate and organize key variables that need to be considered when implementing new programs and practices. Most implementation frameworks share the following set of common themes:

1. Implementation occurs in complex, multilevel systems that include teachers, students, leaders, parents, central office, consultants, universities, and other partners.

2. Implementation unfolds through stages or phases that include pre-implementation exploration, maintenance, and sustainment.

3. Implementation involves bidirectional relationships between settings and evidence-based practices (EBPs):
   a. Both are likely to require some degree of adaptation for implementation.
   b. In EBPs, adaptations focus on components that are not considered critical to effectiveness.
   c. In settings, adaptations focus on aspects of organizational policies, leadership, or infrastructure.

A Work in Progress

REVIEW, REFLECT, RESPOND

Review the three common themes found in all implementation frameworks. To what extent, if any, has your team considered these themes when beginning a change project? Check the appropriate frequency as indicated in the chart below.

Theme	Never	Rarely	Sometimes	Always
1. Implementation occurs in complex, multilevel systems.				
2. Implementation unfolds through stages or phases.				
3. Implementation involves bidirectional relationships between settings and EBPs.				

If these themes were consistently part of your implementation process, what impact might this have on the implementation success?

_____

_____

_____

_____

THE STAGES OF IMPLEMENTATION

The Scaling Up of Evidence-based Practices Center at the University of North Carolina (Fixsen et al., 2013) offers an implementation model that can be adapted and used at the school, district, or state levels. The model includes four stages that are not necessarily linear, and sustainability is embedded in each stage over time. They also recommend that the work be managed by an implementation team consisting of committed individuals from various networks in the school. With the same team membership, members can become quite proficient at the process and navigate effectively forward and backward through the stages. Also of note, a school can be at a full implementation stage with one change initiative and at the exploration stage with another. Each of the stages is described briefly, and a visual model follows.

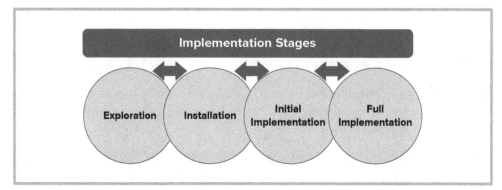

Source: Fixsen et al. (2013).

Exploration Stage: During this stage, the implementation team identifies the need for change, possibly using the initiative inventory discussed in Module 8 to guide the discussion. They also strive to learn more about proposed interventions that may yield better outcomes than current practices, and they explore what it will take to implement the innovation effectively. They discuss how to develop stakeholders and champions of the change initiative and make decisions on proceeding (or not). Furthermore, during this stage, the team examines ways to build readiness for change among stakeholders, as during this stage, stakeholders typically need information and evidence to support their engagement. They need time to process, ask questions, and collaborate with each other on how the change will affect their current practice. Leaders must recognize that readiness for change is not a pre-existing condition. Rather, it must be nurtured and developed by including the essentials listed here in their planning. Accountability for creating readiness lies with the implementation team.

Installation Stage: During this stage, the implementation team determines the resources needed to use an innovation and the resources required to implement the innovation with fidelity, resulting in good outcomes for students. Again, the initiative inventory is a great tool for reallocating funds from ineffective practices that will be de-implemented and redirecting them to new innovations, which promise to provide more benefits for teachers and students. The team may also develop tools to generate evidence on the fidelity of implementation to drive additional professional learning to address teacher misunderstandings or knowledge gaps in the way of deep implementation.

Initial Implementation Stage: During this stage, the innovation is attempted by educators, while those who are supporting them are learning how to lend support for growth with the innovation. This stage most certainly includes trial, error, and adjustment. It is also sometimes referred to as the "awkward stage," as people are learning and growing their confidence with the new practice. Teachers need time together to collaborate and share, and supportive feedback for growth from leaders at all levels is essential for moving staff from the initial implementation stage to the full implementation stage.

Full Implementation Stage: During this stage, the skillful use of an innovation is underway. Teachers have integrated the new practice into their teaching repertoire as a result of consistent support received by established roles, functions, and structures supported by building and potentially district administrations. At the end of the day, it doesn't really matter how great an educational idea or intervention is in principle; what really matters is that it is supported at the deep implementation levels and that its use is evident in the everyday work of people in schools.

 Working on the Work

COMPASS POINTS PROTOCOL

The below graphic and questions are known as a compass protocol. Each direction in the compass rose contains questions for your consideration as you reflect on the implementation process described in this module and assess the possibilities of it working for you and your team. Take notes right on the form. After the questions have been answered, consider the viability of this process for your next change project.

N = Need to Know

What else do you need to know about this idea? What additional information would help you to evaluate things?

W = Worrisome

What do you find worrisome about this idea or information? What is the downside?

E = Excited

What excites you about this idea? What is the upside?

S = Stance and Suggestions

What is your current stance about this idea or information? What are your suggestions for moving forward?

Image credit: Photoco/istockphoto.com

WRITING YOUR IMPLEMENTATION PLAN

On the following pages, you will find a worked example of an implementation plan using the Education Endowment Foundation's implementation planning template. This plan centers on the implementation of retrieval practice in all classrooms, which was also referenced in Module 4. We think this is one of the most effective ways to create an implementation plan for several reasons. It is a plan on a single page and not a 100-page document that no one reads. In addition, this implementation plan format takes a logical and effective approach to implementation of a change practice by using these five steps:

1. Establish the *why* or problem to be solved.

2. Describe the steps or parts to the practice to convey the *what* of the work.

3. Detail the timetable and types of support that will be provided to implementers, which describes the *how* of the work.

4. Consider the *how well* by forecasting the evidence of implementation outcomes from the short to long terms.

5. State the intended learning outcomes for students as a result of engaging in the strategy of retrieval practice. This provides the *and so* part of the plan.

As mentioned earlier in this module, there are various formats and processes for implementation planning. We highlight this format as one way to plan for successful implementation, using both the initiative inventory as shared in Module 8 and the de-implementation process in Module 9.

 A Work in Progress

REFLECTION EXERCISE

Review the example implementation plan on the next two pages. Consider the feasibility of this plan format for your school and respond to the questions that follow.

INTRODUCING RETRIEVAL PRACTICE

Bedlington Academy—Northumberland

Problem (why?)	Intervention Description (what?)	Implementation Activities (how?)	Implementation Outcomes (how well?)	Final Outcomes (and so?)

Teachers
• Cite 'lack of resilience and revision' as key factors in students' underperformance in new examinations.
• Do not understand the evidence in terms of cognitive science and how retrieval practice, including spaced retrieval and interleaving, can support the development of memory.
• Do not incorporate time into lessons for retrieval practice.
• Have been previously trained to teach in methods which favour skills over knowledge.
 	
Students
• Lack resilience to tackle challenging question (higher tariff). This is often due to lack of a secure knowledge.
• Are unable to apply information if they cannot confidently recall the information.
• Need a word hoard of 50,000 to access GCSEs. Poor vocabulary is
	Active ingredient 1
	Connect to previous learning
	• Introduce retrieval practice at the start of every lesson, replacing current 'Connect' (starter) activity, and focusing on spaced retrieval of information from previous lessons.
	• This phase of the lesson to last no more than 5 minutes and to be known as 'SMART Connect'.
	
	Active ingredient 2
	Consolidate immediate learning
	• Introduce retrieval practice at the end of every lesson, replacing current 'Consolidate' (plenary) activity, and to focus on retrieval of information from the lesson which has just taken place.
	• This phase of the lesson to last no more than 5 minutes and to be known as 'SMART Consolidate'.
	
	Active ingredient 3
	Retrieve from memory
	• SMART Connect and SMART Consolidate to be closed book (from memory).
		Feasibility
		• Conduct in-house RCT to test if retrieval practice has a positive impact on vocabulary retention.
		
		Training
		• Consistent, iterative Core CPD over the course of two years to introduce:
		  a. rationale for strategy
		  b. link to evidence
		  c. active ingredients of strategy
		• Core CPD followed up by department CPD to develop subject-specific examples, long term plans and medium term plans.
		
		Communications
		• 'Nudge' emails and verbal reminders regularly to address misconceptions, ensure fidelity and tweak practice (2-3 weekly).
		
		Coaching
		• Year 1: in-school support from subject facilitators and T&L Leaders.
		• Year 2: Research Leads appointed to support and provide ongoing coaching and training in priority subject areas.
			Short term
			Fidelity:
			• Shared understanding of the principles and active ingredients of the intervention.
			• All staff incorporating SMART Connect and SMART Consolidate into lessons.
			
			Reach:
			• All staff are able to identify knowledge gaps in their subject area across the year groups.
			
			Acceptablity:
			• Staff feedback indicates that the strategy is manageable and useful in their classroom.
			
			Medium term
			Fidelity:
			• Staff explicitly identify retrieval practice in planning.
			• All staff using SMART Connect & Consolidate with fidelity (by end of HT4).
				Short term
				• Increased student engagement and confidence in retrieval practice.
				• Improvements in subject-specific vocabulary and core knowledge evident.
				• Students can articulate that there is a consistent approach in lessons to retrieval practice.
				
				Medium term
				• Improved student motivation, cognition and metacognition: students have strategies to develop memory and recall.
				• Student progress data shows improvement in terms of assessment/progress exam scores (by end of HT5).

(Continued)

Problem (why?)	Intervention Description (what?)	Implementation Activities (how?)	Implementation Outcomes (how well?)	Final Outcomes (and so?)
hindering their confidence and progress in examinations. • Are not able to comprehend texts and struggle with higher-level skills such as inference and evaluation. **Attainment** • Low attainment and progress is evident at KS4 (P8 −0.4 in 2017). Disadvantaged pupils perform significantly less well than their non-disadvantaged peers (P8 −0.53 compared with −0.29 for non-disadvantaged). • With bigger and more complex qualifications at every key stage, the demands of the curriculum in terms of knowledge (including knowledge of academic vocabulary) have increased. This deficit is proving a barrier to improved attainment in our school.	**Active ingredient 4** *Quizzing* • **SMART** activities to take the format of quiz questions which test knowledge of factual material, understanding of key vocabulary or application of key knowledge Questions may be multiple choice, true/false or short answer. • Staff draw on a range of formats to present the retrieval practice, including retrieval grids and Powerpoint slide templates. • Answers should be provided and students self-check responses. **Active ingredient 5** *Consistent format* • All staff to refer consistently to these lesson phases using the terms 'SMART Connect and SMART Consolidate'. • SMART logo to be displayed on board/PPT slides during these lesson phases to ensure recognition of these lesson phases and metacognition of the strategies.	**Monitoring** • Lesson drop-ins from week 2 to share good practice and promote fidelity. • Planning check to identify staff who need further support, and implement mentoring plans when required—half termly. • Good practice to be shared and celebrated via a celebration event. **Educational materials** • Logo provided for PPT slides and classroom display. • Copies of relevant evidence sources for all staff.	• Staff are able to adapt future planning to address knowledge gaps based on assessment of it. • Departments are creating resources using a consistent format to explicitly engage students in retrieval practice. • Signs of improving quality of teaching and consistency in planning/approach to retrieval practice. *Reach:* • Staff begin to use and share a range of practical strategies for retrieval practice in lessons. • Retrieval practice becomes an integral aspect of SOWs. **Long term** *Fidelity:* • Responsive and adaptive curriculum and planning. • Consistent, embedded approach to retrieval practice. *Acceptability:* • Staff feel confident and empowered to teach retrieval practice.	**Long term** • Milestone: outcomes data at GCSE (August) shows improvement in P8 and APS score for all student groups. • 2018 outcomes: overall P8 +0.26, A8 43.97 (improved from −0.4 and 37.39 in 2017).

Source: Education Endowment Foundation (n.d.).

In the first column, you can see the problem or *why* of the work is outlined for both teacher and students with evidence to support.

Next, the intervention steps are laid out through "active ingredients," which conveys the *what* of the work. The following section details the implementation activities to support the deep implementation. These activities include professional learning, communication, coaching, and monitoring, which address the *how* of the work.

The final two sections of the plan outline the outcomes for both implementation and learning. Specifically, the implementation outcomes section focuses on the *how well* part of the work by detailing intended outcomes for the short, medium, and long term in the areas of fidelity, reach, and acceptability. Outlining the expected outcomes for learners from the short to long term in column five provides a rationale by detailing the *And so* . . . part of the plan.

REFLECTION

Which elements of the plan format resonate with you?

What challenges might your team face in using this template for your next change project?

What benefits might result from using this format?

ALL IN A DAY'S WORK

Consider the questions that follow and complete the chart to capture your thinking on implementation processes and planning in your school or district. Refer to the exercises you completed to inform your responses.

Which of your current practices on implementation were affirmed in this module?

➡ Place these practices in the KEEP section of the chart.

Which of your current practices conflict with what you have learned in this module?

➡ Place these practices in the STOP section of the chart.

What have you learned in this module that will strengthen your implementation planning for your next change initiative?

➡ Place these practices in the START section of the chart.

ACTIONS	PRACTICES BASED ON MY LEARNING IN THIS MODULE:
KEEP	I will continue to . . .
STOP	I will stop . . .
START	I will start . . .

CONCLUSION

Given all the competing priorities school leaders face today, it is easy to understand that the attention needed for deep implementation of new practices or ideas is lacking. However, sound planning that includes consistent processes for conducting an initiative inventory, identifying practices for de-implementation, and redirecting funds and energy toward the implementation of practices more likely to reach your goals will save time in the long run. School leaders often lament that they rarely experience the thrill or satisfaction of getting to deep implementation of the practices in their schools. "Chasing their tails" is a common refrain we hear. Becoming an agent of change, as described in Mindframe 4, involves purposeful, deliberate planning, and actions on a few things done well and deeply. Thus, for the next change initiative you are considering, revisit this section, share the materials, templates, and processes with your team, and give it a go!

Access resources, tools, and guides
for this module at the companion website:
resources.corwin.com/howleadershipworks

Conclusion

The Work Ahead

Congratulations, you've come to the end of the playbook. Before we let you go, we'd like to provide some summarizing information. First, you are the lead learner, and you have the potential to maximize high-effect practices across the organization. Take this role seriously and do not waiver in your commitment to ensure that every student has a great teacher, not by chance, but by design. Design those experiences for teachers so that they join you on the quest for excellence and strive to be their very best selves.

Second, there are specific actions you can take to establish and maintain the climate of your organization. Monitor the climate and use your implementation and de-implementation skills to ensure that the climate is contributing to learning, by students as well as their teachers. In addition, ensure that conversations between grown-ups are productive and growth producing. This may require that you update the professional learning community processes at your school. It will probably involve increasing the amount and changing the type of feedback provided.

Third, remember you are the leader and manager of change. Do you recall the definition of leadership from the introduction? "Leadership is a process of social influence, which maximizes the efforts of others, toward the achievement of a goal."

We hope that your confidence in leading instructional improvement has increased as a result of your efforts in this book. We provided you with a format and venue, but you did the work.

Now, it's time for you to prioritize. What are the next right steps for your organization? You might consider the Action Priority Matrix from Mind Tools. As they note, you can consider the potential impact and how much effort is required to complete a task. They describe the following four possibilities (Mind Tools, n.d.a.):

> **Quick Wins (High Impact, Low Effort)** are the most attractive projects because they give you a good return with relatively little effort. Focus on these as much as you can.

> **Major Projects (High Impact, High Effort)** are major projects that give good returns, but they are time-consuming. This means that one major project can "crowd out" many quick wins.

> **Fill-Ins (Low Impact, Low Effort)** are tasks that you don't worry about too much. If you have spare time, do them, but drop them or delegate them if something better comes along.

You are the lead learner, and you have the potential to maximize high-effect practices across the organization.

Thankless Tasks (Low Impact, High Effort) are also tasks to try to avoid. Not only do they give little return, but they also soak up time that you should be using on quick wins.

THE ACTION PRIORITY MATRIX

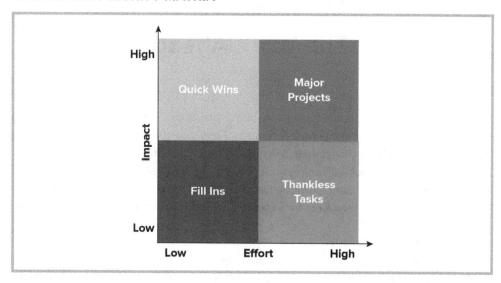

Source: Mind Tools (n.d.a.).

In addition to prioritizing your actions, we hope that you will return to the 10 mindframes and reflect on your responses from the previous exercises. For each of the mindframes listed in the following, mark whether your learning on this mindframe *affirmed* current thinking, *extended* your thinking by adding something new, or *challenged* your thinking by prompting you to consider changes to your current practices. Compare your response now with your thinking from the first module.

Mindframes for Instructional Leadership	Affirmed	Extended	Challenged
1. I am an evaluator of my impact on teacher and student learning.			
2. I see evidence and data as informing my impact and next steps.			
3. I collaborate with peers, teachers, students, and families about my conceptions of progress and my impact.			
4. I am a change agent, and I believe my role is to improve the learning lives of teachers and students.			
5. I embrace challenge, and I support teachers and students in doing the same, not just doing our best.			
6. I foster a culture of feedback where teachers, students, and leaders seek, give, receive, and act on feedback.			

Mindframes for Instructional Leadership	Affirmed	Extended	Challenged
7. I engage as much in dialogue as in monologue.			
8. I explicitly inform teachers and students what successful impact looks like from the outset.			
9. I build relationships and trust to make it safe to make mistakes and learn from others.			
10. I focus on learning and contribute to a shared language of learning.			

As your mindframes grow, and you use these to guide decisions, remember that we are all on a learning journey. We all do what we know how to do. As Maya Angelou taught Oprah, do the best you can until you know better, and when you know better, you do better. Hopefully, you know more now and are that much more prepared to do better.

References

Almarode, J., Fisher, D., & Frey, N. (2021). *How learning works: A playbook*. Corwin.

Angelo, T. A., & Cross, K. P. (1993). *Classroom assessment techniques: A handbook for college teachers* (2nd ed.). John Wiley & Sons.

Bandura, A. (1977). Self-efficacy: Toward a unifying theory of behavioral change. *Psychological Review, 84*(2), 191–215.

Berry, A. (2020). Disrupting to driving: Exploring upper primary teachers' perspectives on student engagement. *Teachers and Teaching, 26*(2), 145–165.

Bryk, A. S., Sebring, P. B., Allensworth, E., Luppescu, S., & Easton, J. Q. (2010). *Organizing schools for improvement: Lessons from Chicago*. Chicago, IL: University of Chicago Press.

Bryk, A., & Schneider, B. (2002). *Trust in schools*. University of Chicago Press.

Buckingham, M. (2016). *First, break all the rules: What the world's greatest managers do differently*. Greenlight.

California Department of Education. (2008). *California preschool learning foundations* (Vol. 1). Author. https://www.cde.ca.gov/sp/cd/re/documents/preschoollf.pdf

Chew, S. L., & Cerbin, W. J. (2020). The cognitive challenges of effective teaching. *Journal of Economic Education, 52*(1), 17–40.

Education Endowment Foundation. (n.d.). *Putting evidence to work: A school's guide to implementation*. https://educationendowmentfoundation.org.uk/public/files/Publications/Implementation/EEF-Example-of-Implementation-Plans.pdf

Education Hub, The. (n.d.). *Feedback checklist*. https://theeducationhub.org.nz/feedback-checklist

Evans, M., Teasdale, R. M., Gannon-Slater, N., La Londe, P. G., Crenshaw, H. L., Greene, J. C., & Schwandt, T. A. (2019). How did that happen? Teachers' explanations for low test scores. *Teachers College Record, 121*(2), 1–40.

Fisher, D., & Frey, N. (2021). Why do students disengage? *Educational Leadership, 79*(1), 76–77.

Fisher, D., Frey, N., Almarode, J., Flories, K., & Nagel, D. (2019). *The PLC+ playbook: A hands-on guide to collectively improving school learning, grades K-12*. Corwin.

Fisher, D., Frey, N., Hattie, J., & Flories, K. (2019). *Learner's notebook. Becoming an assessment-capable visible learner*. Corwin.

Fisher, D., Frey, N., Smith, D., & Hattie, J. (2021a). *The distance learning playbook for school leaders: Leading for engagement and impact in any setting*. Corwin.

Fisher, D., Frey, N., Smith, D., & Hattie, J. (2021b). *Leading the rebound: 20+ must-dos to restart teaching and learning*. Corwin.

Fixsen, D., Blase, K., Horner, R., Sims, B., & Sugai, G. (2013). *Scaling-up brief. Readiness for change*. The State Implementation and Scaling-Up of Evidence-Based Practices Center. UNC Chapel Hill.

Frey, N., Fisher, D., & Almarode, J. (2021). *How tutoring works: Six steps to grow motivation and accelerate student learning*. Corwin.

Fullan, M. (2007). *The new meaning of educational change* (4th ed.) Teachers College Press.

Goddard, R. D. (2003). Relational networks, social trust, and norms: A social capital perspective on students' chances of academic success. *Educational Evaluation & Policy Analysis, 25*(1), 71.

Goddard, R. D., Hoy, W. K., & Hoy, A. W. (2000). Collective teacher efficacy: Its meaning, measure, and impact on student achievement. *American Educational Research Journal, 37*, 479–507.

Good, T. (1987). Two decades of research on teacher expectations. *Journal of Teacher Education, 38*(4), 32–47.

Grissom, J., Egalite, A., & Lindsay, C. (2021). *How principals affect students and schools: A systematic synthesis of two decades of research*. The Wallace Foundation.

Guskey, T. (2020). Flip the script on change. *The Learning Professional, 41*(2). https://learningforward.org/journal/beyond-the-basics/flip-the-script-on-change/

Hall, G., & Hord, S. (2015). *Implementing change: Patterns, principles and potholes* (4th ed.). Pearson.

Hattie, J. (2012). *Visible learning for teachers: Maximizing impact on learning*. Routledge.

Hattie, J. (2015). High-impact leadership. *Educational Leadership, 72*(5), 36–40.

Hattie, J., & Clarke, S. (2019). *Visible learning feedback*. Routledge.

Hattie, J., & Smith, R. (Eds). (2020). *10 mindframes for leaders*. Corwin.

Hattie, J., & Timperley, H. (2007). The power of feedback. *Review of Educational Research, 77*(1), 81–112.

Hattie, J., & Zierer, K. (2018). *10 Mindframes for visible learning*. Routledge.

Hattie, J., & Yates, G. C. R. (2014). Using feedback to promote learning. In Benassi, V. A., Overson, C. E., & Hakala, C. M. (Eds.), *Applying the science of learning in education: Infusing psychological science into the curriculum* (pp. 45–58). American Psychological Association.

Heifetz, R., & Linksy, M. (2002). *Leadership on the Line: Staying alive through the dangers of leading. Harvard Business School Press*. Cambridge.

Hiatt, J. M. (2006). *ADKAR: A model for change in business, government and our community*. Prosci, Inc.

Hord, S. (2004). Professional learning communities: An overview. In S. Hord (Ed.), *Learning together, leading together: Changing schools through professional learning communities* (pp. 5–14). Teachers College Press.

Hoy, W. K., Sweetland, S. W., & Smith, P. A. (2002). Toward an organizational model of achievement in high schools: The significance of collective efficacy. *Education Administration Quarterly, 38*(1), 77–93.

Huberman, M., & Miles, M. B. (1984). *Innovation up close: How school improvement works*. Plenum Press.

Janosz, M. (2012). Outcomes of engagement and engagement as an outcome: Some consensus, divergences, and unanswered questions. In S. L. Christenson, A. L. Reschly, & C. Wylie (Eds.), *Handbook of research on student engagement* (pp. 695–703). Springer Science.

Jerald, C. D. (2007). *Believing and achieving* [Issue brief]. Washington, DC: Center for Comprehensive School Reform and Improvement. Retrieved from https://files.eric.ed.gov/fulltext/ED495708.pdf

Kruse, K. (2013). What is leadership? *Forbes Magazine*. https://www.forbes.com/sites/kevinkruse/2013/04/09/what-is-leadership/?sh=2285e3c15b90

Kruse, K. (2019). *Great leaders have no rules: Contrarian leadership principles to transform your team and business*. Rodale.

Lyon, A. (n.d.). *Implementation science and practice in the education sector*. Substance Abuse and Mental Health Administration, Project Aware. https://education.uw.edu/sites/default/files/Implementation%20Science%20Issue%20Brief%20072617.pdf

Manna, P. (2015). *Developing excellent school principals to advance teaching and learning: Considerations for state policy*. The Wallace Foundation.

Marks, W. (2013). Unpublished doctoral dissertation, University of Wollongong, New South Wales, Australia.

Mind Tools. (n.d.a.). *The action priority matrix*. https://www.mindtools.com/pages/article/newHTE_95.htm

Mind Tools. (n.d.b.). *The four principles of change management*. https://www.mindtools.com/pages/article/newPPM_87.htm

National Implementation Research Network (NIRN). (2017). *"Exploring" with the intiative inventory*. https://nirn.fpg.unc.edu/resources/initiative-inventory

National Implementation Research Network (NIRN). (2020). *Intiative inventory*. https://nirn.fpg.unc.edu/resources/activity-4-2-exploring-initiative-inventory

Northern Territory Government. (2020). *De-implementation guide for the Northern Territory Department of Education*. Author. https://evidenceforlearning.org.au/assets/NT/De-implementation-Guide.pdf

Nuthall, G. A. (2007). *The hidden lives of learners*. New Zealand Council for Educational Research.

Protheroe, N. (2008, May). Teacher efficacy: What is it and does it matter? *Principal*, 42–45.

Purkey, W. W., & Novak, J. M. (1996). *Inviting school success: A self-concept approach to teaching, learning, and democratic practice* (3rd ed.). Wadsworth Publishing.

Robinson, V. M., Lloyd, C. A., & Rowe, K. J. (2008). The impact of leadership on student outcomes: An analysis of the differential effects of leadership types. *Educational Administration Quarterly, 44*(5), 635–674.

Senge, P. M. (2012). *Schools that learn: A fifth discipline fieldbook for educators, parents, and everyone who cares about education* (2nd ed.). Nicholas Brealey Publishing.

Skaalvik, C. (2020). School principal self-efficacy for instructional leadership: Relations with engagement, emotional exhaustion, and motivation to quit. *Social Psychology of Education, 23*, 479–498.

TNTP. (2018). *The opportunity myth: What students can show us about how school is letting them down—and how to fix it*. New York, NY: Author. Retrieved from https://tntp.org/publications/view/student-experiences/the-opportunity-myth

Tschannen-Moran, M. (2004). *Trust matters: Leadership for successful schools*. Jossey-Bass.

Wang, V. M. (2018). Working smarter not harder: Coupling implementation with de-implementation. *HealthCare, 6*(2), 104–107.

Wiggins, G. (2012). Seven keys to effective feedback. *Education Leadership, 70*(1), 10–16.

Index

A SAGE Publishing Company

Helping educators make the greatest impact

CORWIN HAS ONE MISSION: to enhance education through intentional professional learning.

We build long-term relationships with our authors, educators, clients, and associations who partner with us to develop and continuously improve the best evidence-based practices that establish and support lifelong learning.

CORWIN | Fisher & Frey

The PLC+ Books

What makes a powerful and results-driven Professional Learning Community (PLC)? The answer is PLC+, a framework that leads educators to question practices, not just outcomes.

Help your PLC+ group to work wiser, not harder with this practical guide to planning and implementing PLC+ groups in a collaborative setting.

The PLC+ Activator's Guide offers a practical approach and real-life examples that show activators what to expect and how to navigate a successful PLC journey.

To learn more, visit corwin.com/plcbooks

The How "It" Works Books

Rich with resources that support the process of parlaying scientific findings into classroom practice, this playbook offers all the moves teachers need to design learning experiences that work for all students!

How Tutoring Works distills the complexity of strategic moves effective tutors make to build students' confidence and competence.

To learn more, visit corwin.com/howlearningworks

FFN21B82

Put your learning into practice

When you're ready to take your learning deeper, begin your journey with our PD services. Our personalized professional learning workshops are designed for schools or districts who want to engage in high-quality PD with a certified consultant, measure their progress, and evaluate their impact on student learning.

CORWIN PLC+

Empower teacher teams to build collective agency and remove learning barriers

It's not enough to just build teacher agency, we must also focus on the power of the collective. Empowering your PLCs is a step toward becoming better equipped educators with greater credibility to foster successful learners.

Get started at corwin.com/plc

CORWIN Rebound

Build students' confidence and competence with tutoring strategies that spark learning

Effectively address and prevent unfinished learning where students are provided extra time to learn through tutoring. Learn how to establish a relationship of credibility and build students' confidence and relationship to learning.

Get started at corwin.com/tutoringworkshop

CORWIN Visible Learning+®

Translate the science of how we learn into practices for the classroom

Discover how learning works and how this translates into potential for enhancing and accelerating learning. Learn how to develop a shared language of learning and implement the science of learning in schools and classrooms.

Get started at corwin.com/howlearningworksPD

FFN21B82

Learn more about our virtual PD options at corwin.com/virtualpd